Test Preparation Guide for LOMA 356

Investment Principles and Institutional Investing

LOMA (Life Office Management Association, Inc.) is an international association founded in 1924. LOMA is committed to a business partnership with its worldwide members in the insurance and financial services industry to improve their management and operations through quality employee development, research, information sharing, and related products and services. Among LOMA's activities is the sponsorship of several self-study education programs leading to professional designations. These programs include the Fellow, Life Management Institute (FLMI) program and the Fellow, Financial Services Institute (FFSI) program. For more information on all of LOMA's education programs, please visit www.loma.org.

Statement of Purpose: LOMA Educational Programs Testing and Designations

Examinations described in the *LOMA Education and Training Catalog* are designed solely to measure whether students have successfully completed the relevant assigned curriculum, and the attainment of any LOMA designation indicates only that all examinations in the given curriculum have been successfully completed. In no way shall a student's completion of a given LOMA course or attainment of a LOMA designation be construed to mean that LOMA in any way certifies that student's competence, training, or ability to perform any given task. LOMA's examinations are to be used solely for general educational purposes, and no other use of the examinations or programs is authorized or intended by LOMA. Furthermore, it is in no way the intention of the LOMA Curriculum and Examinations staff to describe the standard of appropriate conduct in any field of the insurance and financial services industry, and LOMA expressly repudiates any attempt to so use the curriculum and examinations. Any such assessment of student competence or industry standards of conduct should instead be based on independent professional inquiry and the advice of competent professional counsel.

Test Preparation Guide for LOMA 356

Investment Principles and Institutional Investing

Information in this text may have been changed or updated since its publication date. For current updates, visit www.loma.org.

LOMA Education and Training
Financial Services Institute
Atlanta, Georgia
www.loma.org

PROJECT TEAM:

Authors:	Sean Schaeffer Gilley, FLMI, ACS, AIAA, HIA, CEBS, PAHM, MHP, AIRC, AAPA, ARA, FLHC
	Vivian Heeden, FLMI, CLU, FLHC, ACS, AIAA, PAHM, AIRC, ARA
	Lisa Kozlowski, FLMI, CLU, ACS, AIAA, PAHM, AIRC, ARA, FLHC, AAPA
Project Managers:	Robert H. Hartley, FLMI, ALHC, ACS, CLU, ChFC, RHU, PAHM
Production Manager:	Stephen J. Bollinger, ACS
Print Buyer:	Audrey H. Gregory, ACS
Typesetter:	Kathleen Ryan, FLMI, PCS, FAHM, AIAA, AIRC, ARA
Production Coordinator:	Amy Souwan
Technical Support:	David A. Lewis, FLMI, ACS
Administrative Support:	Marion Markus
Cover Design:	Stephen J. Bollinger

ISBN 1-57974-216-5

Printed in the United States

Contents

The TPG Companion CD-ROM now includes the practice questions and answers found in this booklet (along with answer choice explanations), and a sample exam also with answer choice explanations.

Preface

Before You Begin...

Important Information on How to Study and Prepare for a LOMA Examination

Welcome to the Test Preparation Guide (TPG) for LOMA 356. This learning package was designed by LOMA to complement *Fundamentals of Investing* by Lawrence J. Gitman and Michael D. Joehnk and *Introduction to Institutional Investing* by Susan Conant. The latter text is provided on CD-ROM only. Used along with the texts, this TPG will help you master the course material as you prepare for the LOMA 356 examination. This TPG includes practice exam questions and a full-scale sample examination, both of which are provided in paper form as well as on an enclosed CD-ROM.

The nature of LOMA's self-study program offers two important benefits.

 First, you have the opportunity to learn important job-related information that will help you become a more knowledgeable and valuable employee.

 Second, a self-study program allows you to learn at your own pace and study at times that suit your own schedule.

You may need some help in developing the skills necessary for self study, or you may have some qualms about taking examinations. Even if you're very confident of your study skills, you need to understand what you will be expected to know once you have completed the course and how you can make sure you have mastered the course content. That's why LOMA developed the TPG.

Whether or not you are confident of your study skills and test-taking ability, you owe it to yourself to read through the next two sections in this manual. These introductory sections deal with the two issues mentioned above: effective studying and effective test taking. We've included many practical pointers that will help you study for and take the examination for this course. We have also explained how the TPG is designed and have given you advice on how to use it.

The remainder of the TPG is your guide to mastering the course material. By reading and working through this manual, you not only will discover how to focus your study, but you will also receive valuable practice in applying your knowledge and will be able to gauge your level of mastery of the material.

The TPG is your key to learning success.

Acknowledgments

The TPG for LOMA 356 was designed to provide a comprehensive self-directed learning approach to help students master the information in this course. As with all projects at LOMA, development of the TPG depended upon the combined efforts of many individuals.

Our thanks go to our project manager, Robert H. Hartley, FLMI, ALHC, ACS, CLU, ChFC, RHU, PAHM. Thanks also go to Kathleen Ryan, FLMI, PCS, FAHM, AIAA, AIRC, ARA, for her work typesetting this text and to Amy Souwan for her work coordinating the printing of the TPG and the production of the TPG Companion CD-ROM. In addition, we thank David A. Lewis, FLMI, ACS, who contributed to the technical side of the production process, and Marion Markus for her administrative assistance.

Special thanks go to Ernest L. Martin, Ph.D., FLMI, who is the original author of the introductory material on becoming test-wise.

Sean Schaeffer Gilley, FLMI, ACS, AIAA, HIA, CEBS, PAHM, MHP, AIRC, AAPA, ARA, FLHC
Vivian Heeden, FLMI, CLU, FLHC, ACS, AIAA, PAHM, AIRC, ARA
Lisa Kozlowski, FLMI, CLU, ACS, AIAA, PAHM, AIRC, ARA, FLHC, AAPA

Introduction

Study Tips

This section gives you practical advice on organizing and scheduling your study time so that you can master the assigned material for this course as efficiently and effectively as possible.

Getting Started

Before you begin the process of studying, take time to be sure that you have all the necessary "pieces," that you have evaluated all the resources available, and that you know where you're headed. Imagine finding out you have wasted your time by studying from the wrong edition of a text or for a test that has already been administered.

Materials and Resources

Assigned Text(s). Consult the current *LOMA Education and Training Catalog*[1] listing for this course to make sure you have all assigned texts. Please note that one of the two assigned texts for this course—*Introduction to Institutional Investing*—is provided on CD-ROM only. It will be essential to your success on the examination to read the assigned materials thoroughly. Check your text materials against the catalog listing for the academic year in which you plan to sit for the examination. If there have been multiple editions of assigned materials, be sure that you have the edition that will be used for testing purposes. In all cases, an edition change for a text used in a LOMA Insurance Education Program signals very substantial content changes. Students who study from previous editions of a text to prepare for an examination will be at a severe handicap when they sit for the examination. Although your company's Educational Representative or librarian may make every effort to maintain a current supply of texts for your use, it is your responsibility to secure the proper texts as you begin your study.

Recognize the value of the TPG as a companion to your texts and use it. We designed the TPG to include features that have been shown to significantly improve examination pass rates for the students who use these aids.

Classes. Some companies offer classes to students. The regimen of preparing for classes is helpful to many students, and the chance to review material in a classroom setting reinforces learning. The effectiveness of your study efforts is likely to be enhanced if you use this TPG in combination with classes. LOMA studies have demonstrated the effectiveness of class attendance when it is combined with a study aid such as the TPG. Thus, if you have access to a class, you should participate. However, attending class is not a substitute for reading the assigned material and working through the TPG.

Examination Date. Check the current *LOMA Education and Training Catalog*[1] for the correct examination date for this course.

---

[1] The catalog is available from your LOMA Educational Representative or LOMA's Office of the Registrar. It is also available on LOMA's Web site at www.loma.org.

Preparing for the Examination

The amount of time you need to prepare for an examination depends on you—your comfort with the material and your comfort with your own study skills. Some people spend months studying; others spend a matter of days. We can't really advise you on the length of time you need to study because we don't know your experience with or schooling in the subject matter covered in this course, and we don't know your particular learning style. However, we can offer you a few useful tips.

1. **Start early!** As soon as you enroll for the course, secure the assigned textual materials and begin planning your study schedule.

2. **Evaluate the material.** The examination for which you will sit is based exclusively on the assigned textual materials, ***including information in the body of the text and in the figures, tables, and insights in each chapter***. (Please note that one of the assigned texts for this course is provided on CD-ROM only.) Read each text's preface and scan through each chapter in the text. Note the chapter objectives provided at the beginning of each chapter. Look at the Practice Questions and Sample Exam questions in the TPG. These steps should help you decide how easy or difficult the material seems to you and will help you plan your schedule.

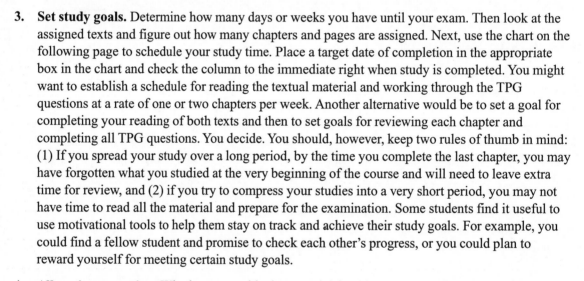

3. **Set study goals.** Determine how many days or weeks you have until your exam. Then look at the assigned texts and figure out how many chapters and pages are assigned. Next, use the chart on the following page to schedule your study time. Place a target date of completion in the appropriate box in the chart and check the column to the immediate right when study is completed. You might want to establish a schedule for reading the textual material and working through the TPG questions at a rate of one or two chapters per week. Another alternative would be to set a goal for completing your reading of both texts and then to set goals for reviewing each chapter and completing all TPG questions. You decide. You should, however, keep two rules of thumb in mind: (1) If you spread your study over a long period, by the time you complete the last chapter, you may have forgotten what you studied at the very beginning of the course and will need to leave extra time for review, and (2) if you try to compress your studies into a very short period, you may not have time to read all the material and prepare for the examination. Some students find it useful to use motivational tools to help them stay on track and achieve their study goals. For example, you could find a fellow student and promise to check each other's progress, or you could plan to reward yourself for meeting certain study goals.

4. **Allow time to review.** Whether you tackle the material for this course one chapter at a time or all at once, you will need some time to review and organize what you have learned. The Practice Questions and Sample Exam in the TPG provide an excellent review of the text material and a measure of your understanding. They also provide you with a preview of the types of questions you are likely to encounter when you take the actual exam.

   A word of caution about reviewing for the examination for this course: Avoid relying on old examinations as study aids. The old tests you have may not be based on the currently assigned materials.

Study Schedule for LOMA 356

	Read Chapter	✓	Complete Practice Questions	✓
Fundamentals of Investing				
Chapter 1				
Chapter 2				
Chapter 3				
Chapter 4				
Chapter 5				
Chapter 6				
Chapter 7				
Chapter 8				
Chapter 9				
Chapter 10				
Chapter 11				
Introduction to Institutional Investing				
Chapter 1				
Chapter 2				
Chapter 3				
Chapter 4				
Chapter 5				
Chapter 6				
Chapter 7				
Chapter 8				
Chapter 9				
Take Sample Examination				

Using the TPG

Studying requires some methodical processes, but the results are worth the effort. Here is one process we recommend for learning the textual material and then preparing for the exam.

1. **Read the learning objectives printed in each text or TPG.** The objectives let you know the relative importance of the subjects covered in the chapter. Keep these objectives in mind as you read the chapter material. Mastering each chapter's learning objectives will help you to be prepared to answer the questions on the examination.

2. **Familiarize yourself with the chapter outline at the beginning of each chapter's Practice Questions in the TPG or in each text's Table of Contents.** Once you know your objectives, take a look at the framework the author has provided for your learning. Each text contains an outline in the Table of Contents. The TPG contains a complete outline at the beginning of each chapter's Practice Questions. Notice the major headings in the outline—these are the broad subject areas covered in the chapter. Then look at the subheadings to see how the material fits together and what the important relationships within the chapter are. You may want to refer to the outline as you read and study, and you may also use it as a review aid when you've finished the chapter.

3. **Read each text chapter at least once.** Some students prefer to read one chapter at a time, stopping to study and review the material using the steps outlined below. Others may wish to read an entire text through once before beginning to review and master the material. Choose the method that best suits you. As you read, be on the lookout for the topics, terms, and concepts that were mentioned in the objectives and outline. Use study techniques such as taking notes on a separate sheet, making notes in the margin of the book, and highlighting or underlining important material. *For the purposes of the examination, you are responsible for information in the body of the text and in the figures, tables, and insights that contain explanatory material in each chapter.*

4. **Answer the Practice Questions in the TPG or on the CD-ROM.** The TPG includes a set of Practice Questions for each chapter of each assigned text. These questions are designed to enhance your test-taking ability by allowing you to practice answering the types of questions that appear on LOMA examinations. These questions may be based entirely on material from the chapter at hand, or they may build upon material from preceding chapters. Do not assume that the number of Practice Questions for a given chapter is indicative of the chapter's relative weight on the examination itself.

   The Practice Questions are presented in two formats. The first is the paper version, and an answer key with text references is located in the Answers to Practice Questions section. For each question you answer incorrectly, you should look up the correct answer in the textbook. The second version of the same Practice Questions is a computer software program found on a CD-ROM located on the inside back cover of this book. Students can use the software version of the Practice Questions as a study aid that provides an analysis of why each answer choice is correct or incorrect.

5. **Take the Sample Exam in the TPG or on the CD-ROM.** Actors have dress rehearsals, and students should too. The best way for you to determine if you are adequately prepared for a LOMA examination is to take the full-scale Sample Exam after you have read the textbook and worked the Practice Questions. The TPG includes one comprehensive examination similar in construction to an actual LOMA examination. This exam is presented in two formats. The first is a paper exam, and an answer key with text references is located in the Text References and Answers to Sample Examination section. The second version of the same Sample Exam is a computer software program found on a CD-ROM located on the inside back cover of this book. The software version of the Sample Exam can be used in two ways: (1) as a straight timed exam with your score furnished at the end or (2) as a study aid that provides analysis of the answer choices with explanations as to why each selection was correct or incorrect.

    Both the Practice Questions and the Sample Exam were developed by staff members in LOMA's Examinations Department using LOMA examination guidelines.

6. **Adapt this process to your individual needs.** Use the techniques that have worked for you in the past and add the study suggestions from this list that you think will help you.

7. **Complete the student survey located at www.loma.org/surveys/stsurvey.htm.** The best way for us to be able to provide the best learning aids to students is to receive feedback from students. Please take a moment to fill out the survey so that we have an understanding of how well this guide helped prepare you for the exam.

Now that you have an understanding of how to plan your study time and how the TPG can assist you in mastering the assigned material, read the following section for tips on becoming "test-wise."

Becoming "Test-Wise"

If you are like most students taking LOMA examinations, you are not a full-time student and have not studied for or taken an exam in many years. Or you may never have taken an examination of the type that will be given for this LOMA program course. In either case, successful performance on a LOMA examination requires more than simply understanding the material; it requires understanding the examination process.

This section is designed to help you become "test-wise." First, we will acquaint you with the type of examinations LOMA administers. We will provide you with some strategies for taking an exam and we'll tell you how to avoid common test-taking mistakes. We'll give you a preview of the types of questions that you will see on LOMA examinations and show you how to use common sense and logic to enhance your chances of answering these questions correctly. And we'll tell you what to do *after* the examination (besides celebrate!).

Examination Structure and Administration

The examination for this LOMA course is offered in paper form twice per year. Students must be enrolled and fees paid well in advance of the scheduled examination administration date, and the examination administration schedule published in the *LOMA Education and Training Catalog* must be strictly adhered to. Students can receive an e-mail grade report approximately three to four weeks after the paper exam administration date. Students may also view exam results by logging into LOMANET and viewing their course history.

The examination for this course is also available on computer. I*STAR (Individually Scheduled Test and Results), LOMA's examination-by-computer system, is part of LOMANET, LOMA's Internet-based education system. The exam is also available at Prometric Testing Centers throughout the United States and Canada.

Students in the many companies that permit students to take I*STAR and/or Prometric exams enjoy the convenience of sitting for examinations at any time of the year, without regard to the strict administration schedule that governs paper examinations. I*STAR and Prometric students receive on-screen notification of examination results immediately upon completion of an examination.

You can enroll for a paper, an I*STAR, or a Prometric exam through LOMANET at www.lomanet.org. Your Educational Representative can inform you of your company's policies and procedures relating to paper, I*STAR, and Prometric exams.

The examination itself contains 75 questions and relies on a 100-point scoring system in which each question is worth $1\frac{1}{3}$ points. A passing score is 70.

What the Examination Will Cover

A test is a sample of knowledge. Limitations of space and testing time make it impossible to test every concept presented in the text materials. You can be certain, however, that the fundamental concepts of a course will be covered in every examination. LOMA emphasizes testing information that is both important and fair to the student.

The current emphasis of LOMA examinations is on putting the student in a decision-making role. In other words, students should be able to demonstrate that they are able to make functional use of the concepts learned. LOMA examinations require students not only to recognize facts or define terms, but also to apply concepts to situations and to draw conclusions. For example, instead of simply asking students to define the concept of net amount at risk, a LOMA examination may require students to calculate the net amount at risk for a particular life insurance policy.

Test-Taking Strategies

There is no substitute for adequate test preparation. Nevertheless, there are techniques that you can use to improve your chances of choosing the correct answer to examination questions and to avoid making test-taking mistakes.

1. **Read the entire question before attempting to answer it, and recognize the key concepts in the stem.** Each examination question contains critical pieces of information, or key concepts, and directions on how to use that information to select the correct answer. For example, a question might ask you for the definition of a term, for a characteristic of a particular product, or for a conclusion based on the "facts" of the situation. Once you have identified the key concepts, you can use them to evaluate the answer choices. The correct answer is the answer that incorporates all of the question's key concepts.

2. **Concentrate on those questions which you are absolutely or reasonably certain you know.** A sound practice in taking any examination is to focus on the questions you can answer confidently and leave until later those questions about which you have some doubt. Go through the entire examination once, answering the questions you can answer and skipping the questions you can't answer. Then go through the test a second time, providing answers to each of the questions you left blank.

3. **If you aren't sure which answer is correct, *make an educated guess.*** If you do not provide an answer to a question, it will automatically be marked incorrect; on the other hand, if you make an educated guess, you have at least a chance of being correct. You can generally use the process of elimination to narrow your choices and improve your chances of selecting the correct response. Start by going back to the key concepts you've identified for the question. If an answer choice does not address one or more of these key concepts, you can eliminate it as a possible response. Following this process almost always allows you to eliminate at least one answer choice. Quite often, the process leaves you with only one answer choice—the correct answer.

4. **Record your answers.** If you are taking a paper exam, record your responses on your answer sheet. Follow the instructions that appear on the examination cover page and on the answer sheet itself in marking your answers on the answer sheet. The answer sheets are graded by machine. If you are taking an electronic exam, record your answers by clicking the round button to the left of the answer choice or by pressing the corresponding number key on the computer keyboard.

5. **Go back through the test and check your answers.** Check the entries that you have recorded on your answer sheet (for a paper exam) or on the computer screen (for an electronic exam). Make sure that all questions have been answered and that your recorded answer choice matches your intended correct response for each question.

An Overview of Question Types Used in LOMA Exams

All of the questions used in LOMA examinations are multiple-choice questions which consist of two parts: (1) an introduction (called a "stem"), which includes key concepts related to the question topic and directions on how to use those key concepts; and (2) a list of possible answer choices. The student's objective is to select the answer choice that correctly satisfies the requirements of the stem.

However, multiple-choice formats vary and questions can range in difficulty from testing simple recognition of terms to testing whether you can manipulate and apply concepts presented in the textual material. The subsection below includes representative examples of the format variations you can expect to see on the examination for this course and some hints on how to approach these questions.

Example 1: Straightforward Multiple-Choice Format

If the premiums for an employer-employee group life insurance contract are paid entirely by the employer, the group insurance plan is said to be

(1) coinsured
(2) vested
(3) nonfunded
(4) noncontributory

Most of the questions in a LOMA examination follow a straightforward multiple-choice format. In these questions, the question "stem" is followed by four answer choices, each of which consists of one term or fact that correctly completes the stem. The question in Example 1 asks for the term used to describe a particular type of insurance plan. The key concepts that will identify which of the four terms presented as answer choices is correct are (1) premiums, (2) employer-employee group life insurance, and (3) payments made solely by the employer. The correct answer is the response that correctly incorporates all of these key concepts. In Example 1, the correct answer is the term that describes a group insurance plan for which the employer pays 100% of the premium and the employees pay nothing.

If you are not sure which answer choice meets these requirements, you can narrow your choices by eliminating any answer choice you know is incorrect. For example, you can eliminate *coinsured* as a possible response because it has nothing to do with premiums. You can also eliminate *nonfunded* because it refers to pension plan funds rather than group life insurance.

Example 2: Multiple-Choice Column Format

Every insurance policy can be classified as being either a contract of indemnity or a valued contract. Dave Holmes is insured by an individual health insurance policy that provides him with basic hospital expense coverage; the policy will pay any hospital expenses Mr. Holmes may incur, subject to a maximum benefit of $300 per day. Mr. Holmes was recently hospitalized for 3 days, and the hospital charged $250 per day for his hospital stay. From the answer choices below, select the response that correctly classifies this insurance contract and that correctly identifies the total benefit amount payable to Mr. Holmes by his insurer in this situation.

	Type of contract	Benefit payable
(1)	valued contract	$750
(2)	valued contract	$900
(3)	contract of indemnity	$750
(4)	contract of indemnity	$900

Example 3: Multiple-Choice Series Format

Amos Reed entered into a contract with the Beacon Insurance Company to sell Beacon's life insurance products. With respect to the roles created by this agency contract, Mr. Reed is considered to be the

(1) principal, and Beacon is the agent

(2) agent, and Beacon is the customer

(3) service representative, and Beacon is the agent

(4) agent, and Beacon is the principal

Column format questions and series format questions require you to know more than one piece of information. As in straightforward multiple-choice questions, column format and series format questions present key concepts and instructions for answering the question. Example 2 instructs you to choose the answer that includes both the correct type of insurance contract and the correct benefit amount payable under the contract. Example 3 instructs you to choose the answer that identifies the roles assumed by an individual and an insurer in an agency relationship.

If you are unsure which answer is correct, or if you know only one piece of information, you can use the process of elimination to narrow the possibilities. For example, if you know that the benefit amount in Example 2 is $750 (3 × daily rate of $250) rather than $900 (3 × maximum benefit of $300), you can eliminate answer choices (2) and (4). You have only to determine whether the contract is a valued contract or a contract of indemnity. In Example 3, if you know that Mr. Reed is an agent, you can eliminate answer choices (1) and (3) and concentrate on determining whether Beacon is the customer or the principal. If you simply don't know, you at least have only two choices remaining from which to make an educated guess.

Example 4: Multiple-Choice "One Correct Statement" Format

The following statements are about the reinstatement of a fixed-premium life insurance policy. Select the answer choice that contains the correct statement.

(1) When such a policy is reinstated, the original policy is canceled and a new policy is issued.

(2) When such a policy is reinstated, the policyowner is charged a higher premium rate based on the insured's attained age.

(3) In most jurisdictions, when such a policy is reinstated, the contestable period expires and the insurer may not contest the policy for any reason.

(4) In order to reinstate such a policy, the policyowner is required to present satisfactory evidence of the insured's continued insurability and to pay all back premiums, plus interest.

This type of multiple-choice question presents a general topic and a series of statements related to that topic. The question stem identifies the topic and the criteria you are to use to evaluate the statements in the answer choices. In Example 4, the topic is reinstatement of a fixed-premium life insurance policy and you are directed to select the one correct statement.

Other questions might ask you to select the one **FALSE** statement in the series. There are no tricks in these questions, but they do require you to *read each answer choice carefully and completely* and to decide whether the answer choice is true or false.

You can narrow your choices on questions such as these by eliminating any answer choices that do not satisfy the criteria presented in the stem. In Example 4, you can safely eliminate all false statements. The more choices you eliminate, the greater your chances are of selecting the correct response.

Example 5: Multiple-Choice "Fill-In" Format

The paragraph below contains two pairs of terms enclosed in parentheses. Determine which term in each pair correctly completes the paragraph. Then select the answer choice containing the two terms that you have chosen.

The maximum annual contribution allowed under a Keogh plan is the **(lesser / greater)** of 25% of annual income or $30,000, and the owner of a Keogh plan **(can / cannot)** deduct this amount from his or her taxable income.

(1) lesser / can

(2) lesser / cannot

(3) greater / can

(4) greater / cannot

The two pieces of information you have to evaluate in this question are (1) the maximum annual contribution allowed under a Keogh plan and (2) the deductibility of plan contributions for Keogh plan owners. Perhaps you know that the maximum annual contribution allowed is the lesser of 25% of annual income or $30,000. This knowledge eliminates (3) and (4) as possible answer choices and increases your odds of answering correctly to 50 percent. All that remains is for you to determine whether the plan contributions are tax deductible.

Example 6: Multiple-Statement Format

The following statement(s) can correctly be made about societal changes in the United States that affect the annuities industry:

    A. The number of people entering retirement is decreasing.
    B. The average length of retirements is decreasing.

       (1) Both A and B
       (2) A only
       (3) B only
       (4) Neither A nor B

In order to answer this question, you have to evaluate *A* and *B* as statements about societal changes in the United States. Suppose you are uncertain about *A*, but you are certain that *B* is incorrect. In this case, you would be left with only (2) and (4) to consider, and your odds of guessing correctly would be 50 percent. To arrive at the correct answer, you need only consider whether *A* is a true statement.

Example 7: "Matching Questions" Format

Questions 18 and 19 are matching questions. Beside each question number is a description of a type of life insurance product. From the following answer choices, choose the term that correctly matches the description of each type of life insurance product.

      (1) Level term life insurance
      (2) Graded-premium whole life insurance
      (3) Continuous-premium whole life insurance
      (4) Limited-payment whole life insurance

18. Rex Larsen's life insurance policy provides a death benefit of $50,000 if his death occurs during the 15-year period in which the policy is in force. Mr. Larsen's annual premium payment remains the same throughout this 15-year period. At the end of the period, his coverage will expire.

19. Walter Fiermann will pay level premiums on his life insurance policy for 20 years. At the end of the 20-year period, Mr. Fiermann's policy will be paid up, but his coverage will continue throughout his life. His policy provides a death benefit of $100,000.

All of the multiple-choice formats discussed so far contain an introductory "stem" and a distinct set of answer choices. Matching questions consist of a description of the general topic under consideration and a set of instructions, followed by two or more questions and a single, common set of answer choices. Your objective is to select the answer choice that matches the term, statement, or situation presented in each question. Matching questions, as used in LOMA examinations, generally cover a relatively large amount of textual material and it is not uncommon for a series of matching questions to be drawn from thematically related material appearing in several textbook chapters. Usually, the number of answer choices exceeds the number of questions. Note, too, that more than four answer choices may be provided.

In order to arrive at the correct answer for matching questions, you should read the first question carefully and identify the key concepts. Then evaluate the answer choices according to the instructions provided in the stem and select the correct answer. Once you have completed the first question in the set, repeat the process for the next question. An important fact to remember about matching questions is that, **unless the directions for the series of matching questions specify otherwise, each answer choice is used only once.** This means that once you have identified the correct answer for one question, you can eliminate that answer choice when you evaluate the next question in the set.

Application Questions and Higher-Level Recognition Questions

As mentioned earlier, LOMA examinations may require students to demonstrate that they can make functional use of the concepts learned. Application questions ask you to manipulate information in such a way as to put into practice a concept that has been covered by the textual materials. In other words, application questions require you to put the knowledge you have gained to work in (1) predicting the consequences of a set of facts, (2) dealing with a real-life situation, or (3) solving a problem. Application questions, therefore, call for a higher level of conceptual skill than mere recognition of a concept, term, or formula.

Higher-level recognition questions do not require you to exercise the same level of question-answering skills that application questions require, but the knowledge required to answer these questions goes beyond basic concept recognition.

In order to highlight the differences between lower-level recognition questions, higher-level recognition questions, and application questions, consider examples 8 through 11.

Example 8: Lower-Level Recognition Question

The two major categories of life insurance products are term life insurance and permanent life insurance. *Permanent* life insurance is a form of insurance that

(1) provides coverage for the insured's lifetime
(2) provides coverage for a limited period of time specified in the policy
(3) pays regular benefits during the insured's entire lifetime
(4) pays benefits only if the insured is still alive at the end of the period specified in the policy

This question requires you merely to recognize one of the characteristics of permanent life insurance. It does not require you to manipulate any information or solve a problem.

Example 9: Higher-Level Recognition Question

Heather Friedman is covered by two group medical expense policies that provide identical benefits. Both policies contain the same deductible and coinsurance requirements. When Ms. Friedman was hospitalized for surgery, the policy designated as her primary plan paid benefits, but the policy designated as her secondary plan paid nothing, even though she filed claims under both policies. This information indicates that Ms. Friedman's secondary plan contains a

(1) split-dollar provision
(2) stop-loss provision
(3) partial disability benefits provision
(4) nonduplication of benefits provision

This question requires no manipulation of information—so it is not an application question—but it does require a higher level of recognition on your part than does Example 8. You not only have to know the definition of a nonduplication of benefits provision to answer this question correctly, but you have to be able to recognize the effect of such a provision in a real world example.

Example 10: Application Question

David Templeton was insured under a $100,000 whole life insurance policy. At the time of Mr. Templeton's death, the policy had a cash value of $10,000 and Mr. Templeton owed a total of $5,000 on an outstanding policy loan. The amount that is payable to the beneficiary of Mr. Templeton's policy is

    (1) $90,000
    (2) $95,000
    (3) $100,000
    (4) $105,000

This application item requires you to manipulate information and calculate a result based on that manipulation. A question of this type will present all of the data that you need to answer the question, and may even include some "red herring" data that does not bear on the correct answer but that might catch a student who hasn't studied.

All calculation questions (like example 10) are application items, but not all application items involve calculations. Consider, for example, the following question:

Example 11: Application Question

William Scott named his children, Trudy and Bob, as primary beneficiaries to share equally in the proceeds of an insurance policy on his life. He also named his wife, Marlene, as the policy's contingent beneficiary. When William died, Trudy and Marlene were the only surviving beneficiaries. In this situation, the death benefit will be paid

    (1) entirely to Trudy
    (2) entirely to Marlene
    (3) to Trudy and Marlene in equal shares
    (4) to Trudy and to Bob's estate in equal shares

This question asks you to predict an outcome based on a given set of facts and is, therefore, an application item.

Microcase-Based Questions

Most LOMA examinations contain at least one "microcase." Each microcase presents a fact situation and a series of questions that serve as the basis for more sustained testing of principles and a greater integration of concepts than you can get in a single question. The microcase fact situation may be presented in one or two short paragraphs, or it may take up half a page or more. Typically, the questions included in the microcase are application or higher-level recognition items.

Examination writers at LOMA attempt to achieve two objectives in every microcase: (1) verisimilitude, or the semblance of actuality, and (2) cross-chapter integration, or the incorporation of concepts from various sections of the textbook on which the examination is based. Microcases, therefore, provide you with the opportunity to bring a number of concepts and a fairly broad spectrum of knowledge to bear on a more realistic situation than can be encountered in a single question.

For example, a microcase might present a person who owns an individual medical expense insurance policy. The microcase situation might provide information on the policy's deductible, coinsurance percentage, and coordination of benefits (COB) provision, and inform you of various medical expenses incurred for various procedures. All of this information in the microcase situation could lead to a series of questions that would require you to know (1) the type of deductible included in the policy, (2) the amount of benefits payable by the insurer, (3) the amount of expenses paid by the insured, (4) whether the insured is eligible for benefits for a type of procedure, and so on.

Even a short microcase situation can provide a foundation for asking a large number of questions that require you to thoroughly understand the underlying concepts and apply those concepts in a complex situation.

As with the increased use of application questions and higher-level recognition items (which we noted above), the use of microcases is an indication that your studies should go beyond the mere memorization of the definitions of key terms and concepts.

Some Test-Taking Myths

No matter how diligently you prepare for the examination, you will be handicapped if you adhere to some test-taking myths that circulate through groups of students with almost self-perpetuating force. Here are a few.

Myth 1:　**Answer choice (1) is the best choice if it is necessary to guess the correct answer to a question because examination writers usually place the correct answer first.**

　　Fact:　The distribution of correct answers to the questions appearing on a LOMA examination is fairly evenly balanced among the available answer choices.

Myth 2:　**There is usually a pattern to the answer key responses.**

　　Fact:　There is no pattern to the order of the correct responses to the questions in a LOMA examination except that the distribution of correct responses is evenly balanced, or relatively so.

Myth 3: **Always choose the longest response to a question because examination writers are careful to qualify the correct answer more than they qualify the incorrect answers.**

Fact: Because the examination writers at LOMA are especially alert to this tendency in examinations in some other testing programs, they take special care to avoid such a pattern. Short answers or average-length answers are just as likely as long answers to be correct.

After the Examination

Paper Examinations

You will not be permitted to take your copy of the examination booklet with you when you leave the examination room. However, the proctor is authorized to return your copy of the examination booklet to you after 24 hours have elapsed. Putting your name on the front of your examination booklet will ensure that you receive the same copy you had while sitting for the examination. If you recorded your selected answers in your examination booklet, you can further reinforce the knowledge that you have gained by looking up the correct answers in the textbook. Contact your Ed Rep to obtain a copy of the text references for the examination. You can also view and download text references at LOMA's Web site at www.loma.org.

Occasionally, students may wish to challenge the validity of certain questions. The basis for such challenges varies; it may be a perception that a question is not clearly worded, or that the correct answer does not accurately reflect the textual passage on which it is based, or that the textual passage is at variance with current practices in the insurance industry. Infrequently, a typographical error may be cited as the basis for a challenge.

If you believe that there is good reason to challenge a test question after you have taken the test, put your challenge in writing and forward it to your Ed Rep, who will forward it to the LOMA Education Division for consideration. Receipt of your challenge will be acknowledged by return mail. Be sure to submit any challenges so that they are received by the date specified in the Education Catalog. Any resulting changes can then be taken into account before answer sheets are scored.

The important point to keep in mind about such challenges is that each one is investigated by the professional staff in the LOMA Education and Training Division. If the staff committee doing the investigation finds that there is merit to the challenge—and the benefit of the doubt is always given to the student—that committee will recommend that the answer key be changed to give credit for more than one answer choice. The effect of such a recommendation is to give the students who chose the allowable responses credit for the challenged questions, regardless of whether the intended correct answer was chosen.

As an additional step, the LOMA Education and Training Division creates various statistical reports designed to call to the staff's attention any irregularities in response patterns to questions. Each such irregularity is investigated in detail to ensure that the reason for it is not some erroneous component of the question. If such an irregularity does lead to discovery of an error in a question, multiple answers will be allowed.

Once final grades are posted, it is not possible to make any changes in them.

I*STAR and Prometric Examinations

Administrative regulations pertaining to electronic examinations do not permit students to keep a record of their answer responses or transport any materials out of the testing room. Exam proctors at I*STAR and Prometric testing facilities are required to collect all notes, scratch paper, etc., from students. These regulations are intended to enhance the security of an examination series available throughout the year.

I*STAR and Prometric students, however, may still avail themselves of the opportunity to challenge test questions. A student who believes that a test question is erroneous should record the question number and convey the challenge immediately to the Ed Rep, who will forward it to LOMA. I*STAR and Prometric examination results are subject to the same extensive statistical checks as are paper examination results.

Practice Questions

CHAPTER 1

The Role and Scope of Investments

Fundamentals of Investing—Chapter One

Chapter Objectives

After studying this chapter, you should be able to

- Understand the meaning of the term *investment* and the factors commonly used to differentiate among types of investments

- Describe the investment process and types of investors

- Discuss the principal types of investment vehicles

- Describe the steps in investing, particularly establishing investment goals, and cite fundamental personal tax considerations

- Discuss investing over the life cycle and investing in different economic environments

- Understand the popular types of short-term investment vehicles

Outline of Major Topics

Investments and the Investment Process
Types of Investments
The Structure of the Investment Process
Investment Vehicles
Short-Term Vehicles
Common Stock
Fixed-Income Securities
Mutual Funds
Derivative Securities
Other Popular Investment Vehicles
Making Investment Plans
Steps in Investing
Considering Personal Taxes
Investing Over the Life Cycle
Investing in Different Economic Environments

Meeting Liquidity Needs: Investing in Short-Term Vehicles
>The Role of Short-Term Vehicles
>Popular Short-Term Investment Vehicles
>Investment Suitability

Practice Questions

1. The paragraph below contains two pairs of terms enclosed in parentheses. Determine which term in each pair correctly completes the paragraph. Then select the answer choice containing the two terms that you have chosen.

    Janet Hitchens purchased shares in a mutual fund. With regard to the type of investment that Ms. Hitchens has made, it is correct to say that Ms. Hitchens invested in (**a portfolio of securities / tangible personal property**), and her investment is an example of the type of investment known as (**a direct / an indirect**) investment.

    (1) a portfolio of securities / a direct
    (2) a portfolio of securities / an indirect
    (3) tangible personal property / a direct
    (4) tangible personal property / an indirect

2. The paragraph below contains an incomplete statement. Select the answer choice containing the term that correctly completes the paragraph.

    Usually, an investment represents either a debt or an equity interest. An investor who purchases _____ typically makes an investment that represents an *equity* interest.

    (1) common stock
    (2) bonds
    (3) options
    (4) derivative securities

3. Governments, businesses, and individuals are the key participants in the investment process. Each participant generally acts as a net supplier or as a net demander of funds. From the answer choices below, select the response that correctly identifies governments, businesses, and individuals as net suppliers or net demanders of funds.

	Governments	Businesses	Individuals
(1)	net suppliers	net suppliers	net demanders
(2)	net suppliers	net demanders	net demanders
(3)	net demanders	net suppliers	net suppliers
(4)	net demanders	net demanders	net suppliers

4. One characteristic of any investment is its liquidity. Liquidity can correctly be defined as the ability of an investment to be converted into cash quickly and with little or no loss in value.

   (1) True
   (2) False

5. Maurice Lalanne purchased 100 shares of stock at $50 per share. Over the next year, he received current income of $35 as a result of owning the stock. He then sold the stock for $52 per share. He did not incur any expenses for either the purchase or sale of this stock. This information indicates that Mr. Lalanne's capital gain on his investment was

   (1) $35
   (2) $165
   (3) $200
   (4) $235

6. A convertible security is a special type of fixed-income obligation that permits the investor to convert the security into

   (1) a security that has an earlier maturity date
   (2) an opportunity to sell or buy another security at a specified price over a given period of time
   (3) a security with a higher interest rate
   (4) a specified number of shares of common stock

7. Mariko Aoki included a number of different types of investment vehicles in her portfolio. In so doing, she made her portfolio less risky than it would have been if she had invested in only one or two investment vehicles. This process of including many different types of investments in a portfolio in order to reduce risk is known as speculation.

   (1) True
   (2) False

8. United States tax law limits the deductions (write-offs) that an investor can take, especially for portfolio and passive income. During 2003, Joseph Leaverton, a resident of the United States, had portfolio income of $300 and passive income of $100. He also incurred $500 of investment-related interest expense, none of which was passive investment expense. Of the $500 of investment-related expenses that Mr. Leaverton incurred, the maximum amount of Mr. Leaverton's allowable deductions associated with portfolio and passive income during 2003 was

   (1) $0
   (2) $200
   (3) $300
   (4) $500

9. Investors tend to follow different investment philosophies as they move through different stages of the life cycle. For investors over the age of 60, the typical investment philosophy favors investments in high-risk common stocks, options, and futures.

   (1) True
   (2) False

10. Interest rates are the single most important variable in determining bond price behavior and returns to investors.

   (1) True
   (2) False

11. Short-term investments are generally considered low in risk. Their primary risk is the risk of default.

   (1) True
   (2) False

12. To fund the national debt, the U.S. Treasury issues a variety of debt securities, including U.S. Treasury bills (T-bills). One characteristic of T-bills is that they are

   (1) not sold in the secondary market
   (2) sold only through noncompetitive bidding
   (3) issued in 12-month and 24-month maturities only
   (4) sold on a discount basis

13. The Beachcliff Insurance Company purchased unsecured promissory notes issued by the Lakeside Corporation, a corporation with a very high credit standing. The notes were sold in multiples of $100,000 and will mature in less than 270 days in order to avoid the need to register the security issue with the Securities and Exchange Commission (SEC). This information indicates that Beachcliff purchased

   (1) banker's acceptances
   (2) financial futures
   (3) commercial paper
   (4) certificates of deposit (CDs)

14. Albert Montoya, a United States resident, invested money in a typical money market mutual fund (MMMF). One true statement about Mr. Montoya's investment is that the MMMF

   (1) provides Mr. Montoya with a fixed, guaranteed return, such as 5%, on his investment
   (2) is insured by the federal government of the United States
   (3) required that Mr. Montoya make an initial investment of at least $100,000
   (4) provides Mr. Montoya with easy access to his funds through check-writing privileges

15. An investor is considering three investments for their safety and their liquidity:

   • A U.S. Treasury bill (91-day)
   • Commercial paper (90-day)
   • Certificate of deposit (3-month, large denomination)

Of these investments, the U.S. Treasury bill has the highest safety and the highest liquidity.

   (1) True
   (2) False

Answers to Practice Questions begin on page 93.
Answer choice explanations are available on the CD-ROM on the inside back cover of this book.

CHAPTER 2

Investment Markets and Transactions

Fundamentals of Investing—Chapter Two

Chapter Objectives

After studying this chapter, you should be able to

- Identify the basic types of securities markets and describe the IPO process

- Explain the characteristics of organized securities exchanges

- Understand the over-the-counter markets, including Nasdaq and alternative trading systems, and the general conditions of securities markets

- Review the importance of global securities markets, their performance, and the investment procedures and risks associated with foreign investments

- Discuss trading hours and the regulation of securities markets

- Explain long purchases and the motives, procedures, and calculations involved in making margin transactions and short sales

Outline of Major Topics

Securities Markets
Types of Securities Markets
Organized Securities Exchanges
The Over-the-Counter Market
Alternative Trading Systems
General Market Conditions: Bull or Bear

Globalization of Securities Markets
Growing Importance of International Markets
International Investment Performance
Ways to Invest in Foreign Securities
Risks of Investing Internationally

Trading Hours and Regulation of Securities Markets
Trading Hours of Securities Markets
Regulation of Securities Markets

Basic Types of Securities Transactions
> Long Purchase
> Margin Trading
> Short Selling

Practice Questions

1. The following statements describe transactions in various types of securities markets. Select the answer choice containing the description of a transaction occurring in a primary market.

   (1) A large institutional investor used a dealer that was not a member of an organized securities exchange to make an over-the-counter purchase of many shares of outstanding common stock at a reduced cost.
   (2) An investor purchased shares of common stock through an initial public offering (IPO).
   (3) An investor purchased shares of outstanding common stock on an organized securities exchange.
   (4) A large institutional investor bypassed a securities dealer and sold shares of outstanding common stock directly to another large institutional investor.

2. The paragraph below contains two pairs of terms enclosed in parentheses. Determine which term in each pair correctly completes the paragraph. Then select the answer choice containing the two terms that you have chosen.

   To help with the sale of the Apollo Corporation's new security issue to the public, Apollo hired the Victory Group. Victory, which is a financial intermediary that specializes in selling new security issues and advising firms with regard to major financial transactions, was solely responsible for purchasing the security issue from Apollo at an agreed-upon price and bearing the risk of reselling it to the public at a profit. This information indicates that Apollo's initial sale of the securities occurred in the (**primary** / **secondary**) market and that Victory functions in this situation as an (**investment bank** / **underwriting syndicate**).

   (1) primary / investment bank
   (2) primary / underwriting syndicate
   (3) secondary / investment bank
   (4) secondary / underwriting syndicate

3. The Schooner Corporation sold new shares of Schooner common stock directly to a selected group of insurance companies and pension funds, without having to register these shares with the Securities and Exchange Commission (SEC). This information indicates that Schooner chose to market its common stock by using

   (1) a rights offering
   (2) a public offering
   (3) an aftermarket
   (4) a private placement

4. One source of information provided to potential investors by brokerage firms is a document that describes the key aspects of a new security and the issuer's financial position and management position. This document, which is a portion of the issuer's registration statement for the new issue, is known as a prospectus.

    (1) True
    (2) False

5. For this question, if answer choices (1) through (3) are all correct, select answer choice (4). Otherwise, select the one correct answer choice.

    One general type of financial market in which securities are bought and sold is a secondary market. With regard to secondary markets, it is correct to say

    (1) that secondary markets include the over-the-counter market, but not organized securities exchanges
    (2) that a secondary market gives securities purchasers liquidity
    (3) that a transaction in a secondary market involves the corporation that issued the security
    (4) all of the above

6. The following statement(s) can correctly be made about organized securities exchanges:

    A. The exchange that accounts for the majority of the total annual dollar volume of shares traded on organized U.S. exchanges is the American Stock Exchange.
    B. Organized securities exchanges operate auction markets in which the flow of buy and sell orders determines the price.

    (1) Both A and B
    (2) A only
    (3) B only
    (4) Neither A nor B

7. An insurance company issued stock that had dual listing. This information indicates that the company listed shares of its stock on more than one organized securities exchange.

    (1) True
    (2) False

8. Connie Smith, a securities dealer, makes a market for Kumquat Corporation stock, which is sold on the over-the-counter (OTC) market. The highest price at which Ms. Smith is willing to purchase shares of Kumquat is $2 per share; the lowest price at which Ms. Smith is willing to sell shares of Kumquat is $3 per share. From the answer choices below, select the response that correctly indicates Ms. Smith's bid price and ask price for Kumquat stock.

	Bid price	Ask price
(1)	$2	$3
(2)	$2	$5
(3)	$3	$2
(4)	$3	$5

9. The National Association of Securities Dealers Automated Quotation (Nasdaq) system reflects the market activity of the fourth market.

   (1) True
   (2) False

10. Conditions in the securities markets are commonly classified as "bull" or "bear," depending on whether securities prices are rising or falling over time. One economic condition that is normally associated with *bull* markets is

   (1) an economic slowdown
   (2) government restraint
   (3) investor optimism
   (4) falling securities prices

11. One way that United States investors can invest in foreign securities is by purchasing dollar-denominated negotiable instruments on the U.S. securities exchanges. These financial instruments, which represent stock of foreign companies that are held in the vaults of banks in the companies' home countries, are known as Yankee bonds.

   (1) True
   (2) False

12. One reason that the United States Congress passed the Investment Company Act of 1940 was to

   (1) abolish the fixed commission schedules of securities brokers
   (2) protect investors against potential abuses by investment advisers by requiring advisers to disclose specific information about themselves to potential investors
   (3) authorize the SEC to regulate the practices and procedures of investment companies
   (4) establish trade associations for the purpose of self-regulation within the securities industry

13. Oscar Cortez used margin trading to purchase 100 shares of Beachside Corporation common stock at $50 per share. The initial margin requirement to purchase the Beachside stock was 70%. If Mr. Cortez purchased this stock by borrowing the maximum amount allowed by the margin requirement, then the total amount that he borrowed in order to purchase the Beachside stock was

   (1) $1,500
   (2) $2,000
   (3) $3,500
   (4) $5,000

14. Monique Adjani used margin trading to purchase 100 shares of Seashell Corporation common stock at $50 per share. The initial margin requirement to purchase the Seashell stock was 70%. One year later, the market value of Ms. Adjani's stock was $60 per share. Assuming no change in the debit balance of Ms. Adjani's margin loan, the effect of the change in the market value of Ms. Adjani's stock is such that one year after purchasing the stock, Ms. Adjani's margin has changed from 70% to

   (1) 17%
   (2) 42%
   (3) 75%
   (4) 90%

15. The paragraph below contains an incomplete statement. Select the answer choice containing the term that correctly completes the paragraph.

One year after Fabienne Moreau used a margin loan to purchase 200 shares of common stock, she discovered that she had paper profits in her margin account. She used a technique known as _____ to use these paper profits to help her purchase additional stock, and she continued to use this technique whenever her margin account contained paper profits.

   (1) debit balancing
   (2) a margin call
   (3) restricted accounting
   (4) pyramiding

16. One reason that an investor would use the type of security transaction known as short selling is to

   (1) seek speculative profits from rising security prices
   (2) purchase a security without working through a broker
   (3) purchase a security without making an initial equity deposit with a broker
   (4) seek speculative profits from falling security prices

Answers to Practice Questions begin on page 93.
Answer choice explanations are available on the CD-ROM on the inside back cover of this book.

CHAPTER 3
Investment Information and Trading

Fundamentals of Investing—Chapter Three

Chapter Objectives

After studying this chapter, you should be able to

■ Identify the major types and sources of traditional and online investment information

■ Explain the characteristics, interpretation, and uses of the commonly cited stock and bond market averages and indexes

■ Review the roles of traditional and online stockbrokers, including the services they provide, selection of a stockbroker, opening an account, and transaction basics

■ Describe the basic types of orders (market, limit, and stop-loss), online transactions, transaction costs, and the legal aspects of investor protection

Outline of Major Topics

Types and Sources of Investment Information
    Types of Information
    Sources of Information
Understanding Market Averages and Indexes
    Stock Market Averages and Indexes
    Bond Market Indicators
Making Securities Transactions
    The Role of Stockbrokers
    Basic Types of Orders
    Online Transactions
    Transaction Costs
    Investor Protection: SIPC and Arbitration

Practice Questions

1. Investment information can be either descriptive or analytical. For a given company, one example of *descriptive* investment information is the

   (1) company's rank for timeliness
   (2) company's financial strength rating
   (3) projected price range and associated annual total returns for the company's stock for the next three years
   (4) company's capital structure

2. In August 2000, the Securities and Exchange Commission (SEC) passed a new rule known as the fair disclosure rule (Regulation FD). One true statement about the fair disclosure rule is that

   (1) the rule makes it illegal to achieve investment gains through using nonpublic information to make profitable securities transactions
   (2) the rule applies to communications with journalists and securities ratings firms
   (3) the rule requires senior executives of a public company to disclose critical information such as earnings forecasts and news of mergers and new products simultaneously to investment professionals and the public via press releases or SEC filings
   (4) violations of the rule are considered fraud and they carry injunctions and fines

3. Investors use stock market averages and indexes to measure the general behavior of stock prices over time. A stock market *index*, such as a Standard and Poor's index, reflects the arithmetic average price behavior of a representative group of stocks at a given point in time.

   (1) True
   (2) False

4. In the United States, the Dow Jones Industrial Average (DJIA) is a stock market average that measures the price behavior of

   (1) 30 high-quality stocks whose behaviors are believed to reflect overall market activity
   (2) all shares traded on the American Stock Exchange (AMEX)
   (3) all shares traded on the New York Stock Exchange (NYSE)
   (4) all actively traded stocks on the NYSE, the AMEX, and the over-the-counter (OTC) market

5. The Dow Jones bond averages reflect the simple mathematical average of the bond yields for each group of bonds included.

   (1) True
   (2) False

6. A discount broker typically executes clients' transactions and provides a full array of brokerage services: providing investment advice and information, holding securities in street name, offering online brokerage services, and extending margin loans.

   (1) True
   (2) False

7. A stockbroker engaged in an illegal and unethical act of causing excessive trading of clients' accounts in order to increase the stockbroker's commissions. This illegal act is referred to as

   (1) insider trading
   (2) shorting-against-the-box
   (3) a red herring
   (4) churning

8. An investor can place a market order or a limit order with a stockbroker. A *market order* is correctly defined as an order to

   (1) buy a stock only if its price reaches or exceeds a specified price before a specified date
   (2) sell a stock only if its price reaches or exceeds a specified price before the investor cancels the order
   (3) buy or sell a stock at the best price available when the investor places the order
   (4) sell a stock when its market price reaches or drops below a specified price

9. In the United States, the Securities Investor Protection Act of 1970 authorized the Securities Investor Protection Corporation (SIPC) to offer limited protection to investors by

   (1) insuring brokerage customer accounts up to a specified amount against the consequences of financial failure of the brokerage firm
   (2) holding arbitration hearings to settle disputes between brokers and investors
   (3) protecting investors against bad investment advice offered by their brokers
   (4) requiring brokerage firms to charge commissions based on fixed-commission schedules

Answers to Practice Questions begin on page 93.
Answer choice explanations are available on the CD-ROM on the inside back cover of this book.

CHAPTER 4

Investment Return and Risk

Fundamentals of Investing—Chapter Four

Chapter Objectives

After studying this chapter, you should be able to

■ Review the concept of return, its components, and the forces that affect the investor's level of return

■ Discuss the time value of money and the calculations involved in finding the future value of various types of cash flows

■ Explain the concept of present value, the procedures for calculating present values, and the use of present value in determining whether an investment is satisfactory

■ Describe real, risk-free, and required returns and the computation and application of holding period return, yield (internal rate of return), and growth rates

■ Discuss the key sources of risk and how they might affect potential investment vehicles

■ Understand the risk of a single asset, risk assessment, and the steps that combine return and risk

Outline of Major Topics

The Concept of Return
    Components of Return
    Why Return Is Important
    Level of Return
The Time Value of Money
    Interest: The Basic Return to Savers
    Computational Aids for Use in Time Value Calculations
    Future Value: An Extension of Compounding
    Future Value of an Annuity
    Present Value: An Extension of Future Value
    The Present Value of a Stream of Returns
    Determining a Satisfactory Investment

Measuring Return

Real, Risk-Free, and Required Returns

Holding Period Return

Yield: The Internal Rate of Return

Finding Growth Rates

Risk: The Other Side of the Coin

Sources of Risk

Risk of a Single Asset

Assessing Risk

Steps in the Decision Process: Combining Return and Risk

Practice Questions

1. At the beginning of the year, Marvin Jennings purchased Peppermint Corporation common stock for $1,000. During the year, he received cash dividends totaling $75 from this stock. At the end of the year, he sold his Peppermint stock for $1,125. This information indicates that the total return Mr. Jennings received on this stock was

    (1) $50
    (2) $75
    (3) $125
    (4) $200

2. Inflation tends to have a positive impact on investment vehicles such as real estate, and a negative impact on vehicles such as stocks and fixed-income securities.

    (1) True
    (2) False

3. If an investment pays interest that is compounded semiannually, then the true rate of interest on the investment will be

    (1) less than the stated interest rate
    (2) less than it would be if the interest rate were a simple interest rate
    (3) greater than it would be if the interest were compounded annually
    (4) greater than it would be if the interest were compounded continuously

4. Exactly two years ago, Kathleen O'Meara deposited $1,000 into a savings account earning 3% interest, compounded annually. Ms. O'Meara made no other deposits to or withdrawals from this account. The amount of money currently in Ms. O'Meara's savings account is

    (1) $1,030.00
    (2) $1,060.00
    (3) $1,060.90
    (4) $1,092.73

5. Winston Murchison has a goal of having $10,000 available in exactly one year. If he earns 6% interest on his investment and if interest is compounded annually, then the amount of money that Mr. Murchison must invest today in order to meet his goal is

    (1) $9,400.00
    (2) $9,433.96
    (3) $9,940.00
    (4) $10,600.00

6. When the discount rate is greater than zero, the present-value interest factor for a single sum is always less than 1.

    (1) True
    (2) False

7. The required return for an investment is correctly defined as

    (1) an investor's estimate of the average rate of inflation in the next year
    (2) the rate of return that an investor can earn on a risk-free investment
    (3) the rate of return that an investor could earn in a perfect world where all outcomes are known and certain
    (4) the rate of return that an investor must earn on the investment in order to be fully compensated for the investment's risk

8. Juanita Huerta purchased a bond for $1,000. When she sold the bond 11 months later, she realized a capital loss of $25. Ms. Huerta also earned $30 interest income on this bond during the holding period. This information indicates that Ms. Huerta's holding period return (HPR) on this bond, excluding returns on reinvested interest income, equaled

    (1) –0.5%
    (2) 0.5%
    (3) 3.0%
    (4) 5.5%

9. If the yield on an investment is equal to or greater than the required return, then the investment is acceptable.

    (1) True
    (2) False

10. The paragraph below contains an incomplete statement. Select the answer choice containing the term that correctly completes the paragraph.

    One source of investment risk is _____, which is concerned specifically with the degree of uncertainty associated with an investment's earnings and the investment's ability to pay investors the returns owed to them.

    (1) market risk
    (2) event risk
    (3) purchasing power risk
    (4) business risk

11. The following information describes the risk profiles associated with two types of investments.

- Investment A is traded in a thin market, in which demand and supply are small. The investment can be quickly sold only at a price that is significantly lower than its purchase price.
- Investment B involves purchasing stock in a company that is financed largely by debt. As a result of its debt financing, the company must meet its fixed-payment obligations before distributing any earnings to stockholders. The firm's inability to meet its debt-related obligations could result in losses for its stockholders.

From the answer choices below, select the response that correctly indicates the primary category of risk associated with each investment.

Investment A	Investment B
(1) event risk	financial risk
(2) financial risk	interest rate risk
(3) liquidity risk	financial risk
(4) liquidity risk	event risk

12. The paragraph below contains two pairs of terms enclosed in parentheses. Determine which term in each pair correctly completes the paragraph. Then select the answer choice containing the two terms that you have chosen.

Jackson Templeton is considering the following investments:

	Average Return	Standard Deviation
Investment A	10%	2.0%
Investment B	10%	2.5%

Mr. Templeton should determine that the coefficient of variation for Investment A is (**0.20 / 5.0**), and that Investment A is (**more / less**) risky than Investment B.

(1) 0.20 / more
(2) 0.20 / less
(3) 5.0 / more
(4) 5.0 / less

13. Three basic risk preference behaviors are known as risk-indifferent, risk-averse, and risk-seeking behaviors. One statement that can correctly be made about these risk preference behaviors is that

(1) most investors are risk averse
(2) a risk-averse investor refuses to accept any risk at all
(3) a risk-seeking investor generally requires an increase in required return in exchange for an increase in risk
(4) a risk-indifferent investor generally will accept a lower return in order to take more risk

Answers to Practice Questions begin on page 93.
Answer choice explanations are available on the CD-ROM on the inside back cover of this book.

CHAPTER 5

Modern Portfolio Concepts

Fundamentals of Investing—Chapter Five

Chapter Objectives

After studying this chapter, you should be able to

- Understand portfolio management objectives and the procedures to calculate the return and standard deviation of a portfolio

- Discuss the concepts of correlation and diversification, and the effectiveness, methods, and benefits of international diversification

- Describe the two components of risk, beta, and the capital asset pricing model (CAPM)

- Review traditional and modern approaches to portfolio management and reconcile them

- Describe the role of investor characteristics and objectives and of portfolio objectives and policies in constructing an investment portfolio

- Summarize why and how investors use an asset allocation scheme to construct an investment portfolio

Outline of Major Topics

Principles of Portfolio Planning
    Portfolio Objectives
    Portfolio Return and Standard Deviation
    Correlation and Diversification
    International Diversification

The Capital Asset Pricing Model (CAPM)
    Components of Risk
    Beta: A Popular Measure of Risk
    The CAPM: Using Beta to Estimate Return

Traditional versus Modern Portfolio
    The Traditional Approach
    Modern Portfolio Theory
    Reconciling the Traditional Approach and MPT

Constructing a Portfolio Using an Asset Allocation Scheme
> Investor Characteristics and Objectives
> Portfolio Objectives and Policies
> Developing an Asset Allocation Scheme

Practice Questions

1. An investor's portfolio includes only two securities, A and B. Whenever the return on Security A increases, the return on Security B decreases. This information indicates that the returns on Securities A and B are

   (1) completely diversified
   (2) positively correlated
   (3) negatively correlated
   (4) uncorrelated

2. For a portfolio combining two risky assets that are perfectly positively correlated, the range of risk is between 0 and the risk of the less risky asset.

   (1) True
   (2) False

3. For the U.S. investor, international diversification typically cannot be achieved by investing in U.S. corporations that do business overseas.

   (1) True
   (2) False

4. The total risk of an asset includes systematic risk. By definition, an asset's systematic risk is the

   (1) portion of the asset's risk that does not respond to market forces
   (2) portion of the asset's risk that is unique to the asset
   (3) portion of the asset's risk that can be reduced through diversification
   (4) product of general forces such as war, inflation, and political events that affect all assets

5. The following statements are about beta, a measure of investment risk. Select the answer choice containing the correct statement.

   (1) Beta measures a stock's diversifiable risk only.
   (2) The beta for the overall market is 0.
   (3) At any given time, the number of stocks having positive betas is roughly equal to the number of stocks having negative betas.
   (4) Stocks with betas of greater than 1.0 tend to be more risky than the market.

6. An investor's portfolio of stocks has a beta of 1.5. If the return on the stock market as a whole increases by 6% over the next 12 months, then the portfolio's beta indicates that the return on this investor's portfolio would increase by

   (1) 4%
   (2) 6%
   (3) 9%
   (4) 12%

7. Investors can use the capital asset pricing model (CAPM) as a tool to assess the impact of a proposed security investment on an investment portfolio's

   (1) cash flow and capital gains
   (2) risk and return
   (3) expected inflation premium and risk-free rate
   (4) present value and future value

8. An investor is considering purchasing a corporation's common stock. The stock has a beta (b_i) of 1.25, the risk-free rate (R_F) is 4%, and the market return (r_m) is 8%. According to the capital asset pricing model (CAPM), the investor's required rate of return (r_i) on this investment is

   (1) 9%
   (2) 11%
   (3) 12%
   (4) 13%

9. Two approaches to portfolio management are modern portfolio theory (MPT) and the traditional approach. Of these two approaches, MPT places greater emphasis on

   (1) using securities analysis techniques to select securities
   (2) diversifying a portfolio across industry lines
   (3) loading up a portfolio with successful well-known stocks
   (4) achieving negative or low-positive correlations among the rates of return for various securities within a portfolio

10. When the coefficient of determination—R^2—is used to evaluate a beta coefficient statistically, the coefficient of determination indicates the percentage of the change in an individual security's return that is explained by its relationship with the market return.

    (1) True
    (2) False

11. Leslie Smart's investment portfolio has 30% allocated to common stock investments, 50% allocated to bond investments, and 20% allocated to short-term securities. When the market values of Ms. Smart's investments shift, she adjusts the portfolio so that these percentages remain constant over time. This information indicates that Ms. Smart uses an asset allocation strategy known as

    (1) the flexible-weightings approach
    (2) the fixed-weightings approach
    (3) tactical asset allocation
    (4) strategic asset allocation

Answers to Practice Questions begin on page 93.
Answer choice explanations are available on the CD-ROM on the inside back cover of this book.

CHAPTER 6

Common Stock Investments

Fundamentals of Investing—Chapter Six

Chapter Objectives

After studying this chapter, you should be able to

- Explain the investment appeal of common stocks and why individuals like to invest in them

- Describe stock returns from a historical perspective and understand how current returns measure up to historical standards of performance

- Discuss the basic features of common stocks, including issue characteristics, stock quotations, and transaction costs

- Understand the different kinds of common stock values

- Discuss common stock dividends, types of dividends, and dividend reinvestment plans

- Describe various types of common stocks, including foreign stocks, and note how stocks can be used as investment vehicles

Outline of Major Topics

What Stocks Have to Offer
    The Appeal of Common Stocks
    Putting Stock Price Behavior in Perspective
    From Stock Prices to Stock Returns
    The Pros and Cons of Stock Ownership

Basic Characteristics of Common Stock
    Common Stock as a Corporate Security
    Buying and Selling Stocks
    Common Stock Values

Common Stock Dividends
    The Dividend Decision
    Types of Dividends
    Dividend Reinvestment Plans

Types and Uses of Common Stock
  Types of Stocks
  Investing in Foreign Stocks
  Alternative Investment Strategies
  Some Popular Investment Styles

Practice Questions

1. Alicia Yount owns 2% of the 10,000 shares of common stock issued by the Maple Corporation. If Maple issues 1,000 additional shares of its common stock in a rights offering, then the number of these new shares that the rights offering will entitle Ms. Yount to purchase is

    (1) 0
    (2) 20
    (3) 180
    (4) 200

* * * * * *

Use the following information to answer questions 2 through 6.

In order to finance his retirement, Andrew Okor invests in stocks that offer attractive current income and/or capital gains over the long run. His primary investment objective is safety of principal. Once he invests in a particular stock, he will hold the stock for at least 15 years, regularly buying additional shares of that stock.

Mr. Okor recently purchased 100 shares of Horizon, Inc., common stock because he was impressed by Horizon's record of dividend payments. Before Mr. Okor purchased the stock, he obtained the following financial information from Horizon's most recent annual report:

  • Net profits after taxes = $3,000,000
  • Number of shares of common stock outstanding = 1,000,000
  • Preferred stock dividends = $600,000

Mr. Okor purchased the Horizon stock prior to September 30, the date of record for a dividend on Horizon common stock. The current market price of Horizon's common stock is $40 per share, and the common stock pays annual dividends of $2 per share. Horizon's stock is classified as a blue-chip stock.

2. The investment strategy that Mr. Okor uses to finance his retirement is an example of

    (1) a speculation strategy
    (2) an aggressive stock management strategy
    (3) a quality long-term growth strategy
    (4) a buy-and-hold strategy

3. The fact that Horizon's common stock is blue-chip stock indicates that, by definition, the stock

    (1) remains stable or even increases when general economic activity is tapering off
    (2) offers the potential for substantial price increase, but only because of some special situation such as the introduction of a promising new product
    (3) has earnings that move up and down with the business cycle
    (4) has a long and stable record of earnings and dividends

4. Horizon's earnings per share (EPS) for the previous year equaled

    (1) $2.00
    (2) $2.40
    (3) $3.00
    (4) $3.60

5. The dividend yield on Horizon's common stock equals

    (1) 5.0%
    (2) 6.0%
    (3) 33.3%
    (4) 41.7%

6. The significance to Mr. Okor of September 30, the date of record, is that this is the date on which

    (1) Horizon's board of directors must determine the amount of dividend it will pay
    (2) Horizon's board of directors must decide whether it will declare a dividend
    (3) Mr. Okor must be a registered shareholder of Horizon in order to be entitled to receive Horizon's dividend
    (4) Horizon must mail dividend checks to holders of record of Horizon common stock

          *   *   *   *   *   *

7. Ten years ago, Molly Wong purchased 150 shares of Midfield Corporation common stock. Since her purchase, the only changes to Ms. Wong's Midfield share holdings have occurred as the result of two stock splits: a 3-for-2 stock split five years ago and a 2-for-1 stock split last year. This information indicates that the number of shares of Midfield common stock that Ms. Wong currently owns is

    (1) 50
    (2) 175
    (3) 450
    (4) 626

8. The New York Stock Exchange (NYSE) stock quotation for the Lakeview Corporation for Monday, May 17, showed a net change of +0.40, a high price of 66.56, and a last (closing) price of 62.70. This information indicates that the closing price of Lakeview's common stock on Friday, May 14, was

    (1) 62.30
    (2) 63.10
    (3) 66.16
    (4) 66.96

9. One way to describe the worth of a share of common stock is by its book value. A common stock's book value represents the

    (1) amount that investors believe the stock is worth
    (2) difference between the market price and the par value of the common stock
    (3) amount of common stockholders' equity in a firm
    (4) prevailing market price of the common stock issue

10. For a stockholder who participates in a dividend reinvestment plan (DRIP), the reinvested dividends are similar to stock dividends, in that they are not taxed until the stocks are actually sold.

    (1) True
    (2) False

11. When making a direct investment in foreign stock, the investor wants the value of both the foreign stock and the foreign currency to increase.

    (1) True
    (2) False

12. Justin Witherspoon, an individual investor, relies heavily on technical analysis and focuses on relative price movements in the market, rather than on the fundamentals of the underlying companies. He looks at stock price, earnings, and other indicators to identify signs that a stock's price is about to soar or fall relative to the market. This information indicates that Mr. Witherspoon's investment style is known as

    (1) momentum investing
    (2) growth investing
    (3) sector rotation
    (4) value investing

Answers to Practice Questions begin on page 93.
Answer choice explanations are available on the CD-ROM on the inside back cover of this book.

CHAPTER 7
Analytical Dimensions of Stock Selection

Fundamentals of Investing—Chapter Seven

Chapter Objectives

After studying this chapter, you should be able to

- Discuss the security analysis process, including its goals and functions

- Appreciate the purpose and contributions of economic analysis

- Describe industry analysis and note how it is used

- Demonstrate a basic understanding of fundamental analysis and why it is used

- Calculate a variety of financial ratios and describe how financial statement analysis is used to gauge the financial vitality of a company

- Use various financial measures to assess a company's performance, and explain how the insights derived form the basic input for the valuation process

Outline of Major Topics

Security Analysis
> Principles of Security Analysis
> Who Needs Security Analysis in an Efficient Market?

Economic Analysis
> Economic Analysis and the Business Cycle
> Key Economic Factors
> Developing an Economic Outlook

Industry Analysis
> Key Issues
> Developing an Industry Outlook

Fundamental Analysis
> The Concept
> Financial Statements
> Key Financial Ratios
> Interpreting the Numbers

Practice Questions

1. Traditional security analysis consists of three types of analysis: economic analysis, industry analysis, and fundamental analysis. Of these three types, *fundamental analysis* is the type of analysis that is most concerned with the study of the

    (1) general outlook for a particular industry
    (2) financial condition and operating results of a specific company
    (3) general state of the economy and its potential effects on security returns
    (4) bond and stock markets and the various economic forces at work in the marketplace

    *　*　*　*　*　*

Use the following information for the Candelabra Corporation to answer questions 2 through 6.

BALANCE SHEET
December 31, 2003

Cash	$ 10,000	Notes payable	$ 6,000
Accounts receivable	100,000	Accounts payable	84,000
Inventories	160,000	Total current liabilities	$ 90,000
Total current assets	$270,000	Long-term debt	80,000
Long-term assets	60,000	Stockholders' equity	160,000
		Total liabilities and	
Total assets	$330,000	stockholders' equity	$330,000

Additional financial information about Candelabra:

Annual sales = $600,000
Net profit after taxes = $20,000
Dividends per share = $2
Earnings per share = $4
Market price of Candelabra common stock = $50

2. For 2003, Candelabra had a current ratio of

    (1) 1.22
    (2) 1.67
    (3) 3.00
    (4) 3.38

3. For 2003, Candelabra's accounts receivable turnover was

    (1) 2.70
    (2) 3.30
    (3) 6.00
    (4) 10.00

4. In 2003, Candelabra's return on assets (ROA) was

    (1) 4.00%
    (2) 6.06%
    (3) 8.00%
    (4) 12.50%

5. Candelabra's debt-equity ratio for 2003 was

    (1) 0.50
    (2) 0.53
    (3) 0.55
    (4) 0.89

6. In 2003, Candelabra's dividend payout ratio was

    (1) 0.33
    (2) 0.48
    (3) 0.50
    (4) 2.00

*   *   *   *   *   *

7. The paragraph below contains an incomplete statement. Select the answer choice containing the term that correctly completes the paragraph.

Investors who use economic analysis as part of security analysis may refer to a specific measure of the business cycle known as the _____, which represents the market value of all goods and services produced in a country over the period of a year.

    (1) index of leading indicators
    (2) index of industrial production
    (3) consumer price index
    (4) gross domestic product (GDP)

8. The mature growth phase of an industry's growth cycle is the stage most influenced by economic developments.

    (1) True
    (2) False

9. A firm's balance sheet is a financial statement that provides a summary of the firm's cash flow and other events that caused changes in its cash position.

    (1) True
    (2) False

10. Activity ratios compare a company's sales to various asset categories in order to measure how well the company is utilizing its assets. An example of an activity ratio is the

(1) price-to-book value ratio
(2) net profit margin ratio
(3) times interest earned ratio
(4) inventory turnover ratio

CHAPTER

8 Stock Valuation and Investment Decisions

Fundamentals of Investing—Chapter Eight

Chapter Objectives

After studying this chapter, you should be able to

- Explain the role that a company's future plays in the stock valuation process and develop a forecast of a stock's expected cash flow

- Discuss the concepts of intrinsic value and required rates of return, and note how they are used

- Determine the underlying value of a stock using the dividend valuation model, as well as other present value- and price/earnings-based stock valuation models

- Gain a basic appreciation of the procedures used to value different types of stocks, from traditional dividend-paying shares to new-economy stocks with their extreme price/earnings ratios

- Describe the key attributes of technical analysis, including some popular measures and procedures used to assess the market

- Discuss the idea of random walks and efficient markets and note the challenges these theories hold for the stock valuation process

Outline of Major Topics

Valuation: Obtaining a Standard of Performance
Valuing a Company and Its Future
Developing an Estimate of Future Behavior
The Valuation Process
Stock Valuation Models
The Dividend Valuation Model
Some Alternatives to the DVM
Determining Expected Return
The Price/Earnings (P/E) Approach
Putting a Value on Tech Stocks

Technical Analysis
Principles of Market Analysis
Measuring the Market
Using Technical Analysis
Charting

Random Walks and Efficient Markets
A Brief Historical Overview
Why Should Markets Be Efficient?
Levels of Market Efficiency
Possible Implications
So Who Is Right?

Practice Questions

1. Most companies with high price/earnings (P/E) ratios have high dividend payouts.

   (1) True
   (2) False

2. An investor used the dividend valuation model (DVM) to determine the value of a share of stock. This investor is following the principle which states that the value of a share of stock is primarily a function of its

   (1) approximate yield
   (2) future sales price
   (3) future dividends
   (4) current market price

3. The investment department of Oleander Financial Services will use the constant growth dividend valuation model to compute the value of a share of Azalea Corporation common stock. Oleander's investment department knows the following information about the Azalea stock:

   - The dividends are projected to increase at a constant rate (g) of 6%
   - The next year's dividend (D_1) is expected to be $4 per share
   - The discount rate (required rate of return) (k) is 10%

   According to the constant growth model, the Azalea common stock should sell for

   (1) $25.00
   (2) $40.00
   (3) $66.67
   (4) $100.00

4.   In the dividends-and-earnings (D&E) approach to valuing stock, the single most important and most difficult variable to project is the price/earnings (P/E) multiple.

   (1) True
   (2) False

5.   Investors use technical indicators to assess some of the key elements of stock market behavior and thus gain valuable insights into the general condition of the market and, perhaps, where the market is headed over the next few months. The technical indicator known as the theory of contrary opinion evaluates the

   (1) relative strength or weakness of market volume
   (2) number of stocks that advance or decline in price
   (3) number of stocks sold short in the market at any given point in time
   (4) amount and type of odd-lot trading

6.   One characteristic of the point-and-figure charts that are used by technical analysts is that these charts typically

   (1) include both a time dimension and a price dimension
   (2) cover a maximum time span of one week
   (3) record all changes in the prices of the stocks being measured
   (4) keep track of emerging price patterns in the market

7.   The paragraph below contains an incomplete statement. Select the answer choice containing the term that correctly completes the paragraph.

   The _____ states that security analysis is unable to help predict future stock market behavior because stock price movements are unpredictable.

   (1) chart formation theory
   (2) burn rate theory
   (3) random walk hypothesis
   (4) leverage hypothesis

8.   One basic theory of the behavior of efficient markets is known as the efficient markets hypothesis (EMH). One tenet of the EMH is that

   (1) information becomes available to different types of investors at different times, depending on an investor's ability to pay for the information
   (2) investors react quickly and accurately to new information, causing securities prices to adjust quickly and, on average, accurately
   (3) information on events that impact the stock market tends to be disseminated at evenly spaced intervals
   (4) one individual investor, acting alone, has the potential to affect the prices of securities

9. The efficient markets hypothesis (EMH) is the basic theory describing the behavior of active, efficient markets in disseminating information among investors. There are three forms of the EMH: weak, semi-strong, and strong. With regard to the dissemination of information about the market, the *strong* form of the EMH holds that

    (1) investors cannot use any particular information, public or private, to consistently earn abnormal profits because stock prices immediately adjust to any information, even if it is not available to every investor
    (2) past information on stock prices is essential in order to predict future price changes
    (3) stock prices adjust to information only when the information is available to most investors
    (4) investors can consistently earn abnormally large profits by using only publicly available information

Answers to Practice Questions begin on page 93.
Answer choice explanations are available on the CD-ROM on the inside back cover of this book.

CHAPTER 9

Bond Investments

Fundamentals of Investing—Chapter Nine

Chapter Objectives

After studying this chapter, you should be able to

- Explain the basic investment attributes of bonds and their use as investment vehicles

- Describe the essential features of a bond and distinguish among different types of call, refunding, and sinking-fund provisions

- Describe the relationship between bond prices and yields, and explain why some bonds are more volatile than others

- Identify the different types of bonds and the kinds of investment objectives these securities can fulfill

- Discuss the global nature of the bond market and the difference between dollar-denominated and non-dollar-denominated foreign bonds

- Describe the role that bond ratings play in the market and the quotation system used with various types of bonds

Outline of Major Topics

Why Invest in Bonds
    Putting Bond Market Performance in Perspective
    Exposure to Risk
Essential Features of a Bond
    Bond Interest and Principal
    Maturity Date
    Call Features—Let the Buyer Beware!
    Sinking Funds
    Secured or Unsecured Debt
    Principles of Bond Price Behavior
The Market for Debt Securities
    Major Market Segments
    Specialty Issues
    A Global View of the Bond Market

Trading Bonds
    Bond Ratings
    Reading the Quotes

Practice Questions

1.   The paragraph below contains two pairs of terms enclosed in parentheses. Determine which term in each pair correctly completes the paragraph. Then select the answer choice containing the two terms that you have chosen.

Bond prices are strongly influenced by market interest rates. As a general rule, interest rates and bond prices move in (**the same direction / opposite directions**). For example, if the market interest rate is 8%, then the price of a 6% bond most likely will be (**greater / less**) than the bond's par value.

    (1) the same direction / greater
    (2) the same direction / less
    (3) opposite directions / greater
    (4) opposite directions / less

2.   The following statement(s) can correctly be made about bonds as an investment vehicle:

    A. Bondholders are entitled to the rights and privileges that go along with an ownership position in the company that issued the bonds.
    B. As a general rule, adding bonds to a portfolio will have a much greater impact on lowering risk than on increasing returns.

        (1) Both A and B
        (2) A only
        (3) B only
        (4) Neither A nor B

3.   The risk that a bond will be retired or prepaid by the issuer before its scheduled maturity date is known as

    (1) business/financial risk
    (2) purchasing power risk
    (3) liquidity risk
    (4) call risk

4.   A sinking fund provision in a bond stipulates that the issuer will repay the entire principal amount of a bond issue on the stated maturity date.

    (1) True
    (2) False

Use the following information to answer questions 5 and 6.

The Artifact Company issued $1,000 bonds with a coupon rate of 6% that specify a single maturity date that is 20 years from the date of issue. The bond issue carries a provision that prohibits prepayment for 10 years, after which time Artifact is free to retire the issue. The bond issue is backed by financial assets owned by Artifact but held in trust by a third party.

Four years after Artifact issued the bonds, the prevailing market interest rate was 4%.

5. With regard to the different types of bonds, it most likely is correct to say that Artifact's bonds are an example of

    (1) serial bonds
    (2) noncallable bonds
    (3) unsecured bonds
    (4) senior bonds

6. A bond can be sold as a premium bond or as a discount bond. Four years after issue, when market interest rates were 4%, Artifact's bond most likely would sell at a

    (1) premium, which means that the bond would sell for more than $1,000
    (2) premium, which means that the bond would sell for less than $1,000
    (3) discount, which means that the bond would sell for more than $1,000
    (4) discount, which means that the bond would sell for less than $1,000

                    *   *   *   *   *   *

7. Bonds with lower coupons and/or longer maturities respond more vigorously to changes in market interest rates than do bonds with higher coupons and/or shorter maturities.

    (1) True
    (2) False

8. Treasury bonds are issued with maturities of 2, 5, and 10 years, whereas Treasury notes carry 30-year maturities.

    (1) True
    (2) False

9. The government of State A in the United States issued bonds to help fund the construction of a toll road. These bonds will be serviced by the income produced from the toll road. This information indicates that State A issued a type of

    (1) agency bond known as a revenue bond
    (2) agency bond known as a general obligation bond
    (3) municipal bond known as a revenue bond
    (4) municipal bond known as a general obligation bond

10. Assume that a municipal bond offers a yield of 6.4%. Considering only *federal* taxes, an investor in the 36% tax bracket would have to find a fully taxable bond with a yield of 10% in order to match the return of this municipal bond.

    (1) True
    (2) False

11. One type of specialty bond issued in the United States is the zero-coupon bond. One characteristic of zero-coupon bonds is that these bonds

    (1) offer little potential for capital gains, as compared to other types of bond issues
    (2) make periodic interest payments to the bondholder
    (3) are sold at a deep discount from their par value
    (4) allow the bondholder to defer taxes on interest income until the bond's maturity date

12. The following statement(s) can correctly be made about mortgage-backed securities:

    A. As with other types of bonds, mortgage-backed securities provide investors with periodic interest income and the principal is paid in a lump sum at maturity.
    B. Mortgage-backed securities are structured so that they are not subject to loan prepayment risk.

    (1) Both A and B
    (2) A only
    (3) B only
    (4) Neither A nor B

13. The paragraph below contains two pairs of terms enclosed in parentheses. Determine which term in each pair correctly completes the paragraph. Then select the answer choice containing the two terms that you have chosen.

Investment bankers can use a process known as (**subordination** / **securitization**) to bundle some type of debt-linked asset, such as loans or receivables, and then sell to investors the right to receive all or part of the future payments made on that debt. The resulting investments, which are often backed by pools of auto loans and credit card bills, are known as (**asset-backed securities** / **debentures**).

    (1) subordination / asset-backed securities
    (2) subordination / debentures
    (3) securitization / asset-backed securities
    (4) securitization / debentures

14. From the standpoint of United States investors, one advantage to purchasing foreign-pay bonds is that these bonds

    (1) are registered with the Securities and Exchange Commission (SEC)
    (2) are not subject to currency risk
    (3) are not subject to interest rate risk
    (4) have a positive diversification effect on bond portfolios

15. The rating that a bond receives from a rating agency at the time of issue is not subject to review and is carried by the bond until maturity.

    (1) True
    (2) False

16. The paragraph below contains two pairs of terms enclosed in parentheses. Determine which term in each pair correctly completes the paragraph. Then select the answer choice containing the two terms that you have chosen.

    Investors can make certain assumptions based on the rating that a bond issue receives from a rating agency. Investment-grade bonds receive the highest set of ratings, followed by medium-grade investment bonds, speculative issues (junk bonds), and issues in default or in danger of default. All other factors being equal, the higher the rating, the (**higher** / **lower**) the yield. Investors can also assume that investment-grade bonds are likely to be (**more** / **less**) interest-sensitive than junk bonds.

    (1) higher / more
    (2) higher / less
    (3) lower / more
    (4) lower / less

Answers to Practice Questions begin on page 93.
Answer choice explanations are available on the CD-ROM on the inside back cover of this book.

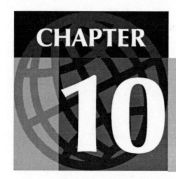

CHAPTER 10 Bond Valuation and Analysis

Fundamentals of Investing—Chapter Ten

Chapter Objectives

After studying this chapter, you should be able to

■ Explain the behavior of market interest rates, and identify the forces that cause interest rates to move

■ Describe the term structure of interest rates, and note how these so-called yield curves can be used by investors

■ Understand how bonds are valued in the marketplace

■ Describe the various measures of yield and return, and explain how these standards of performance are used in bond valuation

■ Understand the basic concept of duration, how it can be measured, and its use in the management of bond portfolios

■ Discuss various bond investment strategies and the different ways these securities can be used by investors

Outline of Major Topics

The Behavior of Market Interest Rates
Keeping Tabs on Market Interest Rates
What Causes Rates to Move?
The Term Structure of Interest Rates and Yield Curves
The Pricing of Bonds
Annual Compounding
Semiannual Compounding
Measures of Yield and Return
Current Yield
Yield-to-Maturity
Yield-to-Call
Expected Return
Valuing a Bond

Duration and Immunization
> The Concept of Duration
> Measuring Duration
> Bond Duration and Price Volatility
> Uses of Bond Duration Measures

Bond Investment Strategies
> Passive Strategies
> Trading on Forecasted Interest Rate Behavior
> Bond Swaps

Practice Questions

1. A bond's risk premium is one element of the equation used to determine the bond's required rate of return. The risk premium takes into account all of the following factors **EXCEPT** the

    (1) characteristics of the bond issuer
    (2) issue's term-to-maturity
    (3) expected inflation premium
    (4) bond's call features and rating

2. Yield spreads, or interest rate differentials, exist among the various bond market sectors. Correct statements about yield spreads within the bond market include

    A. That, within the municipal bond sector, general obligation bonds typically yield more than revenue bonds
    B. That freely callable bonds generally provide higher returns than do bonds with other types of call features, at least at date of issue
    C. That the yield on low-coupon bonds is generally less than the yield on high-coupon bonds

    > (1) A, B, and C
    > (2) A and B only
    > (3) B and C only
    > (4) C only

3. As a general rule, interest rates tend to rise during periods of economic expansion and fall during periods when economic activity contracts.

    (1) True
    (2) False

4. In bond markets, the most common yield curve is downward-sloping, which means that yields tend to decrease with longer maturities.

    (1) True
    (2) False

5. The paragraph below contains three pairs of terms enclosed in parentheses. Determine which term in each pair correctly completes the paragraph. Then select the answer choice containing the three terms that you have chosen.

In bond markets, several theories help explain the shape of the yield curve and its behavior over time. According to the expectations hypothesis, an expectation of an increase in the rate of inflation will result in (**an upward-sloping / a downward-sloping**) yield curve. The market segmentation theory explains the yield curve on the basis of maturity preferences of lenders and investors, such that, when supply outstrips demand for long-term loans and demand for short-term loans is higher than the available supply of funds, the yield curve will tend to be (**upward-sloping / downward-sloping**). According to the liquidity preference theory, investors must be motivated, via higher interest rates, to invest in bonds with (**longer / shorter**) maturities.

    (1) an upward-sloping / upward-sloping / longer
    (2) an upward-sloping / downward-sloping / longer
    (3) a downward-sloping / upward-sloping / shorter
    (4) a downward-sloping / downward-sloping / shorter

6. A bond's price is equal to the present value of the annuity of the bond's annual interest income.

    (1) True
    (2) False

*　*　*　*　*　*

Use the following information to answer questions 7 and 8.

	Present value interest factors (*PVIFs*)					Present value interest factors for an annuity (*PVIFAs*)			
Period	4%	5%	8%	10%	Period	4%	5%	8%	10%
10	0.676	0.614	0.463	0.386	10	8.111	7.722	6.710	6.145
20	0.456	0.377	0.215	0.149	20	13.590	12.462	9.818	8.514

Consider a 10-year bond with a par value of $1,000 and a 10% coupon rate. Mallory Sharpe used annual compounding to calculate the price at which the bond would yield 8%. Then Ms. Sharpe repeated the calculation using semiannual compounding.

7. Using *annual* compounding, Ms. Sharpe most likely determined that the price at which the bond would yield 8% is equal to

    (1) $877.60
    (2) $1,134.00
    (3) $1,196.80
    (4) $1,815.00

8. To calculate the bond's price using semiannual compounding, Ms. Sharpe must make some modifications to the calculation. Adjustments that Ms. Sharpe must make to her original calculation to allow for *semiannual*, rather than annual, compounding include

    A. Doubling the number of periods
    B. Doubling the amount of the annual interest payment
    C. Using a required return of 4%

        (1) A, B, and C
        (2) A and B only
        (3) A and C only
        (4) B only
        (5) C only

        *   *   *   *   *   *

9. One statement that can correctly be made about the bond valuation measure known as yield-to-maturity (YTM), or promised yield, is that YTM

    (1) considers only the bond's price appreciation and principal payments
    (2) can gauge the return on a single issue, but it cannot track the behavior of the bond market in general
    (3) assumes that the investor holds a bond over a period of time that is less than the remaining life of the issue
    (4) assumes that the investor reinvests all coupon income at an average rate equal to or greater than the computed promised yield

10. Consider a $1,000 10-year zero-coupon bond that can be purchased for $386. Using the present value interest factors listed below, and assuming annual compounding, it is correct to say that the yield for this bond is approximately 10%.

    Present value interest factors for $1 (*PVIFs*)

Period	8%	9%	10%	11%
10	0.463	0.422	0.386	0.352
20	0.215	0.178	0.149	0.124

    (1) True
    (2) False

11. Consider a 20-year, 10% deferred-call bond with a 10-year deferred call period. The bond's par value is $1,000 and the bond has 6 years to go before it becomes callable at a call price of $1,085. With regard to the measure of bond yield known as yield-to-call (YTC), it most likely is correct to say that, in this situation, YTC

    (1) is applicable only if the bond's current market price is higher than $1,000
    (2) defines the investment horizon as 14 years for the purposes of the calculation
    (3) uses the bond's par value to determine the present value of the principal to be received at maturity
    (4) defines the investment horizon as 20 years for the purposes of the calculation

12. Correct statements about the measure of bond return known as expected return, or realized yield, include

    A. That the investment horizon used in the calculation is the bond's term to maturity

    B. That this measure is based, in part, on the investor's estimate of future market interest rates

        (1) Both A and B
        (2) A only
        (3) B only
        (4) Neither A nor B

13. The paragraph below contains three pairs of terms enclosed in parentheses. Determine which term in each pair correctly completes the paragraph. Then select the answer choice containing the three terms that you have chosen.

A bond's coupon, maturity, and yield interact to produce the issue's measure of duration. In general, higher coupons result in (**shorter** / **longer**) durations; longer maturities mean (**shorter** / **longer**) durations; and higher yields (YTMs) lead to (**shorter** / **longer**) durations.

        (1) shorter / shorter / longer
        (2) shorter / longer / shorter
        (3) longer / longer / shorter
        (4) longer / shorter / longer

14. The following statement(s) can correctly be made about the measure of duration, which is used to indicate how a bond will react in different interest rate environments:

    A. One disadvantage of using duration is that it does not consider all of the bond's cash flows or the time value of money.

    B. Duration assumes that the investor reinvests all of the bond's periodic coupon payments at the same rate over time.

        (1) Both A and B
        (2) A only
        (3) B only
        (4) Neither A nor B

15. A bond portfolio is said to be immunized when the weighted-average duration of the portfolio exactly equals the investment horizon.

        (1) True
        (2) False

16. The following statements describe bondholders' use of various types of investment strategies. Select the answer choice containing the description of a bondholder who is using the investment strategy known as *bond ladders.*

   (1) When making investment decisions, Carlos Lopez relies heavily on his ability to forecast future interest rates. In anticipation of declining interest rates, Mr. Lopez purchased moderately discounted, investment-grade bonds with low coupon rates. Should interest rates start to level off and move up, Mr. Lopez would shift his money out of long, discounted bonds and into high-yielding issues with short maturities. His goal is to earn as much as possible in as short a time as possible.

   (2) Khalid Rashad reduced the $5,000 tax liability he incurred from the profitable sale of some security holdings by selling a bond issue that had undergone a $5,000 capital loss and replacing it with a comparable obligation.

   (3) Jill Kubek uses an investment strategy that involves liquidating a low-coupon bond holding and simultaneously buying a comparable higher-coupon issue with the same maturity. Ms. Kubek hopes to realize an immediate pickup of current yield and yield-to-maturity.

   (4) Erin Young purchased fixed-income bonds in equal amounts of 3-, 5-, 7-, and 10-year issues. When each of these issues matures, she will use the resulting income to purchase a new 10-year note. By rolling the matured issues into new 10-year issues every few years, Ms. Young hopes to lessen the impact of swings in market interest rates.

Answers to Practice Questions begin on page 93.
Answer choice explanations are available on the CD-ROM on the inside back cover of this book.

CHAPTER 11

Mutual Funds: Professionally Managed Investment Portfolios

Fundamentals of Investing—Chapter Eleven

Chapter Objectives

After studying this chapter, you should be able to

- Describe the basic features of mutual funds, and note what they have to offer as investment vehicles

- Distinguish between open- and closed-end funds, as well as other types of professionally managed investment companies, and discuss the various types of fund loads, fees, and charges

- Discuss the types of funds available and the variety of investment objectives these funds seek to fulfill

- Discuss the investor services offered by mutual funds and how these services can fit into an investment program

- Gain an appreciation of the investor uses of mutual funds, along with the variables to consider when assessing and selecting funds for investment purposes

- Identify the sources of return and compute the rate of return earned on a mutual fund investment

Outline of Major Topics

The Mutual Fund Phenomenon
    An Overview of Mutual Funds
    Open- or Closed-End Funds
    Exchange-Traded Funds
    Some Important Considerations
    Other Types of Investment Companies
Types of Funds and Services
    Types of Mutual Funds
    Investor Services

Investing in Mutual Funds
Investor Uses of Mutual Funds
The Selection Process
Investing in Closed-End Funds
Measuring Performance

Practice Questions

1. The following statements describe advantages that mutual funds offer to individual investors. Three of the statements are true, and one of the statements is false. Select the answer choice containing the **FALSE** statement.

    (1) Investing in mutual funds allows individual investors to benefit from a much greater degree of portfolio diversification than they would be able to achieve by investing on their own.
    (2) Mutual funds are actively managed by full-time professionals, giving individual investors access to investment expertise and relieving them of day-to-day management chores.
    (3) Investors in mutual funds generally can expect to consistently outperform the market over the long term.
    (4) Mutual fund investments can be started without a large capital outlay from the investor.

2. For each mutual fund, various functions—investing, record keeping, safekeeping, and others—are split among one or more entities. This separation of duties is designed to protect the mutual fund investor/shareholder. Of the parties included in the structure of a mutual fund, the custodian is the party that

    (1) keeps track of purchase and redemption requests from the shareholders
    (2) runs the portfolio and makes the buy and sell decisions on securities
    (3) analyzes securities and looks for viable investment candidates
    (4) physically safeguards the securities and other assets of the fund

3. In the United States, a mutual fund is essentially a tax-exempt organization, so long as it meets certain conditions.

    (1) True
    (2) False

Use the following information to answer questions 4 through 7.

Susan Netzger purchased shares in the Opal Mutual Fund, a typical open-end, no-load mutual fund that restricts its investments to stocks of firms in the technology industry. Ms. Netzger purchased her shares at a price per share equal to the fund's net asset value (NAV). The NAV at which she purchased the shares was determined based on the following fund data: assets of $50,000,000, liabilities of $400,000, and 1,000,000 shares outstanding.

4. The fact that Opal operates as a typical open-end mutual fund most likely indicates that

   (1) Opal operates with a fixed number of shares outstanding and cannot issue new shares
   (2) Opal has a fixed amount of capital to invest
   (3) Opal will buy back Ms. Netzger's shares whenever she decides to sell them
   (4) Opal's shares are traded in the over-the-counter market or on some other exchange

5. According to this information, Ms. Netzger purchased her Opal shares at an NAV of

   (1) $0.40
   (2) $49.60
   (3) $50.00
   (4) $50.40

6. Because Opal is a typical no-load fund, Opal

   (1) cannot charge Ms. Netzger a management fee
   (2) cannot charge Ms. Netzger a 12(b)-1 fee
   (3) consists of an unmanaged pool of investments that is held under the terms of a trust agreement
   (4) did not charge Ms. Netzger a sales commission for her purchase of the fund's shares

7. Based on its focus on the technology industry, Opal can correctly be categorized as

   (1) a sector fund
   (2) a money fund
   (3) a balanced fund
   (4) an index fund

*   *   *   *   *   *

8. Exchange-traded funds (ETFs) combine some of the operating characteristics of open-end funds and some of closed-end funds. Characteristics that ETFs share with *closed-end* funds include

   A. That ETFs typically are traded on listed exchanges
   B. That the ETF distributor cannot create new shares or redeem old shares

   (1) Both A and B
   (2) A only
   (3) B only
   (4) Neither A nor B

9. Investing in value funds generally is considered to be riskier than investing in growth or aggressive growth funds.

   (1) True
   (2) False

10. Every mutual fund has a particular investment objective, and a mutual fund is commonly categorized according to its investment policy and objective. The following statements are about different types of mutual funds. Select the answer choice containing the correct statement.

   (1) Index funds tend to have high levels of realized capital gains.
   (2) The primary focus of equity-income funds is capital appreciation.
   (3) Investing in a bond mutual fund is generally more liquid than investing directly in bonds.
   (4) Growth funds focus on investing in stocks that provide high dividends and high current income.

11. Whereas most mutual funds concentrate on one type of investment, whether stocks, bonds, or money market securities, asset allocation funds put money into all these markets.

   (1) True
   (2) False

12. United States investors in international mutual funds, which invest exclusively in foreign securities, obtain capital gains when the value of the dollar *rises* relative to other currencies.

   (1) True
   (2) False

13. As a general rule, mutual funds that have low dividends and low asset turnover have higher tax-efficiency ratings.

   (1) True
   (2) False

14. Caleb Winter purchased a relatively large number of shares of a closed-end fund (CEF) for $8 per share. The fund's NAV is $10. Correct statements about this situation include

   A. That Mr. Winter purchased the shares at a discount of 20%
   B. That Mr. Winter's purchase of a large number of shares of this fund most likely could not influence the share's market value
   C. That Mr. Winter most likely purchased his shares directly from the CEF itself

      (1) A, B, and C
      (2) A and C only
      (3) B and C
      (4) A only
      (5) B only

15. The following information relates to the performance of one share of the Diamond Mutual Fund, a no-load, open-end fund, over a one-year holding period:

Price (NAV) at the beginning of the year $25.00
Price (NAV) at the end of the year $29.00
Dividends received $0.50
Capital gains distributions $1.50

According to this information, the one-year holding period return (HPR) for Diamond was approximately

(1) 14%
(2) 16%
(3) 21%
(4) 24%

Answers to Practice Questions begin on page 93.
Answer choice explanations are available on the CD-ROM on the inside back cover of this book.

CHAPTER 1

Investments in a Financial Services Company

Introduction to Institutional Investing—Chapter One

Chapter Objectives

After studying this chapter, you should be able to

- Describe the hierarchy that directs the activities of a financial services company's investment operation and identify the people who are responsible for setting the company's investment policy

- Describe the role of the investment committee in a financial institution

- Explain the basic purpose of asset-liability management in financial services companies

- Describe the responsibilities of investment professionals, including portfolio managers, asset traders, economists, and various types of investment analysts

- Describe the steps in an asset trade and explain the asset trader's duty of *best execution*

Outline of Major Topics

Organizational Design for Investments
Overview of Investment Units
Asset-Liability Management
Marketing Investment Services
Investment Administration
Investment Accounting and Financial Reporting
Investment Operations
    Portfolio Management
    Asset Management Units
    Investment Professionals and Their Jobs

Practice Questions

1. The investment committee is a standing committee of a financial services company's board of directors.

    (1) True
    (2) False

2. An investment committee that exercises its authority on a ratification basis must approve an investment before the investment can be purchased.

    (1) True
    (2) False

3. Investment department activities can be divided into several categories, including asset-liability management, investment administration, investment accounting and financial reporting, and investment operations. Activities such as portfolio management, asset valuation, credit monitoring, and asset trading are typically categorized under

    (1) asset-liability management
    (2) investment administration
    (3) investment accounting and financial reporting
    (4) investment operations

4. The marketing of investment advisory services to institutional clients usually requires that a company be registered as a financial adviser.

    (1) True
    (2) False

5. Reporting account performance to individual and institutional customers is an investment function that is typically performed by the portfolio management unit.

    (1) True
    (2) False

6. The Cornerstone Insurance Company holds many different types of investments, including bonds, mortgage-backed securities, leases, and common stock. All of these investments can be categorized as fixed-income investments **EXCEPT** for the

    (1) bonds
    (2) mortgage-backed securities
    (3) leases
    (4) common stock

7. Jackson Ladd works in the investment division of a financial services company. Mr. Ladd studies issuers of securities and makes buy, sell, or hold recommendations as to future trading activity in these stocks. According to this information, Mr. Ladd's role in the investment function can best be described as that of

    (1) a portfolio manager
    (2) an investment accountant
    (3) an investment analyst
    (4) an asset manager

8. Leslie Day, a portfolio manager for the Pinwheel Financial Services Company, gave a purchase order for a particular stock to Gerald Blake. Mr. Blake, one of several investment professionals at Pinwheel who executes purchases and sales of securities, works only with Ms. Day and does not get purchase or sell orders from any of Pinwheel's other portfolio managers. With regard to the organization of Pinwheel's investment function, it most likely is correct to say that Mr. Blake is an

    (1) equities analyst working in a centralized trading environment
    (2) equities analyst working in a decentralized trading environment
    (3) asset trader working in a centralized trading environment
    (4) asset trader working in a decentralized trading environment

9. In investment terminology, the term *best execution* refers to the verification that the person requesting a transaction has the authority to make the transaction.

    (1) True
    (2) False

Answers to Practice Questions begin on page 93.
Answer choice explanations are available on the CD-ROM on the inside back cover of this book.

CHAPTER 2
Portfolio Management

Introduction to Institutional Investing—Chapter Two

Chapter Objectives

After studying this chapter, you should be able to

- Describe important elements of an investment policy and differentiate between investment policy and investment strategy

- Compare and contrast conservative versus aggressive investment strategies; passive versus active portfolio management strategies

- Explain the purpose of portfolio immunization and the use of duration and cash-flow matching

- Discuss the measurement and evaluation of investment portfolio performance

- Describe the content and purpose of the Global Investment Performance Standards® (GIPS®)

Outline of Major Topics

Investment Policy
Investment Objectives
> Examples of Investment Objectives
> Requirements for Review of Objectives, Performance Evaluation,
>> and Performance Measurement

Investment Philosophy and Views of Market Efficiency
Portfolio Management Strategies
> Active Portfolio Management
> Passive Portfolio Management
> Portfolio Styles

Investment Performance Measurement, Analysis, and Reporting
> Selection of Appropriate Benchmarks
> Market Indexes as Benchmarks
> Portfolios as Benchmarks
> Benchmarks Derived from Models
> Performance Reporting Standards

Practice Questions

1. A statement of investment policy for a financial services company commonly specifies

    A. Prohibitions against participation in specified activities—for example, trading in commodities or lending of securities
    B. A system and a schedule for monitoring the investment program's compliance with the investment policy

    (1) Both A and B
    (2) A only
    (3) B only
    (4) Neither A nor B

2. A portfolio benchmark states the limits on the portion of a portfolio or asset class that may be invested in a stated category.

    (1) True
    (2) False

3. A statement of portfolio objectives should contain requirements for periodic review of portfolio performance and for review of the objectives themselves.

    (1) True
    (2) False

4. The paragraph below contains two pairs of terms enclosed in parentheses. Determine which term in each pair correctly completes the paragraph. Then select the answer choice containing the two terms that you have chosen.

    A company's investment (**philosophy** / **strategy**) describes the company's view of the investment environment and the company's strategic strengths in that environment. A company that views markets for the exchange of assets as (**efficient** / **inefficient**) considers that market prices for assets do not immediately and fully reflect all pertinent information, and that expertise and diligent effort on the part of investment professionals can enable a company to identify assets that are undervalued in the markets.

    (1) philosophy / efficient
    (2) philosophy / inefficient
    (3) strategy / efficient
    (4) strategy / inefficient

5. A conservative investment strategy requires a higher level of risk tolerance than does an aggressive investment strategy.

    (1) True
    (2) False

6. Correct statements about active portfolio management include that an active portfolio management style

    A. Reflects a bias toward the belief that markets are perfectly efficient
    B. Involves incurring more commissions on trades and more costs for research than does a passive management style

    (1) Both A and B
    (2) A only
    (3) B only
    (4) Neither A nor B

7. The practice of using portfolio management strategies such as cash flow matching and duration matching, which are designed to protect fixed-income portfolios against losses triggered by fluctuations in market interest rates, is known, by definition, as

    (1) portfolio diversification
    (2) portfolio asset allocation
    (3) portfolio performance attribution analysis
    (4) portfolio immunization

8. The paragraph below contains two pairs of terms enclosed in parentheses. Determine which term in each pair correctly completes the paragraph. Then select the answer choice containing the two terms that you have chosen.

    Portfolios can be grouped according to their investment styles. An investment portfolio designed to replicate the asset mix of the S&P 500 is an example of an (**income / index**) portfolio that uses (**an active / a passive**) portfolio management approach.

    (1) income / an active
    (2) income / a passive
    (3) index / an active
    (4) index / a passive

9. A growth portfolio typically invests primarily in corporate bonds.

    (1) True
    (2) False

10. Fred Kluytman is a portfolio manager with the Prairie Life Insurance Company. Last year, Mr. Kluytman was required to meet a benchmark percentage return of 5.125% on the stock portfolio that he managed. This benchmark is based on a stock market index. Prairie provided the following incentives for Mr. Kluytman to achieve a minimum spread over the established benchmark.

> Level 1 bonus: the portfolio manager attained 25 basis points over the benchmark
> Level 2 bonus: the portfolio manager attained 100 basis points over the benchmark
> Level 3 bonus: the portfolio manager attained 200 basis points over the benchmark

The total percentage return last year on the stock portfolio Mr. Kluytman managed was 5.425%. Mr. Kluytman's portfolio also had a high tracking error relative to the benchmark. The following statement(s) can correctly be made about this situation:

A. The portfolio Mr. Kluytman manages most likely was less risky than the benchmark.
B. Mr. Kluytman most likely earned a Level 3 bonus based on his portfolio's total percentage return.

    (1) Both A and B
    (2) A only
    (3) B only
    (4) Neither A nor B

11. The Association for Investment Management Research (AIMR) has created a standardized set of investment performance calculation standards called the Global Investment Performance Standards (GIPS). GIPS contains requirements and recommendations covering

A. Input data
B. Calculation methodology
C. Composite portfolio construction
D. Disclosures
E. Presentation and reporting

    (1) A, B, C, D, and E
    (2) A, B, and C only
    (3) B, C, and D only
    (4) D and E only

12. In order to certify that they have complied with GIPS, companies must use approved methods for calculating investment performance returns. GIPS-compliant methods for calculating investment performance returns include

A. The modified Dietz method of total return
B. Net asset value (NAV) portfolio performance calculation

    (1) Both A and B
    (2) A only
    (3) B only
    (4) Neither A nor B

Answers to Practice Questions begin on page 93.
Answer choice explanations are available on the CD-ROM on the inside back cover of this book.

CHAPTER 3

Insurance Company Investment Portfolios

Introduction to Institutional Investing—Chapter Three

Chapter Objectives

After studying this chapter, you should be able to

- Discuss special aspects of managing insurance portfolios, including investment limitations and general account segmentation

- Differentiate between (1) a life insurance company's general account and its segments and (2) a life insurance company's separate accounts and their subaccounts

- Explain the outcomes of portfolio segmentation for life insurance companies

- Differentiate between a centralized and a decentralized plan of asset allocation for the general account of an insurance company

- Explain the need for investment income allocation and describe three alternative methods for allocating investment income

Outline of Major Topics

Major Portfolios of Insurance Companies
    The General Account
    The Separate Accounts
General Account Segmentation
Approaches to Asset Allocation
    Centralized Asset Allocation for the General Account
    Decentralized Asset Allocation for the General Account
Investment Income Allocation Methods
    Investment Segmentation Method
    Mean Liabilities Method
    Investment Year Method

Practice Questions

1. The paragraph below contains two pairs of terms enclosed in parentheses. Determine which term in each pair correctly completes the paragraph. Then select the answer choice containing the two terms that you have chosen.

    Companies incorporated as life insurance companies have two main types of portfolios: general account portfolios and separate account portfolios. The assets that support an insurance company's contractual obligations to owners of the company's guaranteed products are held in the insurer's (**general** / **separate**) account. These are investments for which the (**insurer** / **client**) bears the investment risk.

    (1) general / insurer
    (2) general / client
    (3) separate / insurer
    (4) separate / client

2. An insurer's separate account is an investment company registered with the Securities and Exchange Commission (SEC).

    (1) True
    (2) False

3. The following statement(s) can correctly be made about the management of an insurance company's general account:

    A. Insurance laws limit the manner in which insurers invest and the assets that insurers may choose to hold.
    B. Under insurance accounting practices, the valuations of liabilities tend to be lower and the valuations of assets tend to be higher than under other accounting systems.

    (1) Both A and B
    (2) A only
    (3) B only
    (4) Neither A nor B

4. In its regulation of the investment practices of insurance companies, the National Association of Insurance Commissioners (NAIC) has developed two approaches to limiting the investment risks undertaken by insurers: the Investments of Insurers Model Act—Defined Standards Version and the Investments of Insurers Model Act—Defined Limits Version. The Defined Standards Version of this act gives insurers specific and narrowly defined investment limits rather than allowing them discretion in balancing portfolio risk exposures.

    (1) True
    (2) False

5. Establishing portfolio segments and allocating new investments and investment income to those segments are crucial elements of managing general account investments for a life insurance company. Asset allocation for the general account can follow a centralized or a decentralized approach. As compared to a decentralized approach to asset allocation, a *centralized* approach

    (1) permits product line portfolio managers to better address the unique needs of their product's customers
    (2) ensures that each product line is allowed to develop its own investment policy
    (3) ensures that overall investment selection for the general account is made on a sound and consistent basis
    (4) gives portfolio managers more control over investment performance for their own product lines

6. Insurers use a number of investment income allocation methods to assign investment revenues to specific portfolio segments in their general accounts. Under one type of investment income allocation method, an insurer uses the cash flows of a product line to purchase specific assets for that line. Each product line is treated as though the product line owned specified investments, with the investment income from each asset being allocated to the line that acquired the asset. This type of investment income allocation method, under which different product lines can apply distinct investment strategies, is known as the

    (1) investment segmentation method
    (2) mean liabilities method
    (3) investment year method
    (4) modified Dietz method

Answers to Practice Questions begin on page 93.
Answer choice explanations are available on the CD-ROM on the inside back cover of this book.

CHAPTER 4

Assets and Asset Mixes

Introduction to Institutional Investing—Chapter Four

Chapter Objectives

After studying this chapter, you should be able to

- Explain quality classes for bonds and credit quality for mortgages

- Discuss characteristics of venture capital and limited partnerships

- Discuss the relative shares of stocks, bonds, mortgages, and real estate in life insurance company portfolios

- Discuss the relative shares of stocks and bonds in property/casualty insurance company portfolios

- Explain the importance of investment earnings for life insurers relative to their premiums from annuities, life insurance, and health insurance

- Explain the role of investments in the cash flow cycle for life insurance companies

Outline of Major Topics

Asset Classes
    Bond Characteristics and Bond Holdings
    Commercial and Residential Mortgages
    Equity Investments
Asset Mixes
Industry Asset Mixes
Investment Income Sources for Insurers
Earnings of Life Insurers
Investments in the Life Insurance Company's Cash-Flow Cycle
    Examples of Cash Inflows from Customers
    Examples of Cash Inflows from Investments
    Examples of Cash Outflows for Investments
    Examples of Cash Outflows for Product Obligations and Company Expenses

Practice Questions

1. Some bonds are traded in the public bond markets, whereas others are placed through a private placement. In comparing these two methods, it is generally correct to say that *private placements* tend to

    (1) contain fewer protective covenants than do otherwise comparable public bonds
    (2) be more liquid than are otherwise comparable public bonds
    (3) be more labor intensive for the investor than are otherwise comparable public bonds
    (4) produce lower yields than do otherwise comparable public bonds

2. In general, life insurers concentrate their general account bond investments in short-term bonds.

    (1) True
    (2) False

3. For this question, if answer choices (1) through (3) are all correct, select answer choice (4). Otherwise, select the one correct answer choice.

    The following statement(s) can correctly be made about private rating agencies and the National Association of Insurance Commissioners (NAIC), both of which develop and publish credit ratings on bond issuers:

    (1) The NAIC is the only source of quality ratings for private placement bonds.
    (2) Ratings from the private rating agencies, such as Moody's and Standard & Poor's, embed more information on public bonds than do the NAIC ratings.
    (3) The NAIC rating system consists of six rating levels that encompass all investment-grade securities.
    (4) All of these statements are correct.

4. The following statements are about mortgages, which are an important investment category for financial services companies. Select the answer choice containing the correct statement.

    (1) Most of the mortgages held in life insurance company portfolios are restructured mortgages.
    (2) A mortgage represents an unsecured debt.
    (3) The greatest share of mortgages held in the general account portfolios of insurance companies is in commercial mortgages and commercial mortgage-backed securities.
    (4) In the United States, commercial mortgages commonly have longer terms to maturity than do residential mortgages.

5. The paragraph below contains two pairs of terms enclosed in parentheses. Determine which term in each pair correctly completes the paragraph. Then select the answer choice containing the two terms that you have chosen.

    For insurance companies, stocks are the largest asset class held in the (**general** / **separate**) account portfolios. Most of the stock held by insurance companies is (**common** / **preferred**) stock.

    (1) general / common
    (2) general / preferred
    (3) separate / common
    (4) separate / preferred

6. An insurance company can invest venture capital by participating in a limited partnership arrangement. As the limited partner, the insurance company does not assume responsibility for the debts of the business beyond the level of its cash contribution.

    (1) True
    (2) False

7. Financial institutions have different patterns of investing in various asset classes, based in part on finding the asset mix that best matches the institution's obligations to its customers. Consider the following categories of financial institutions:

    - Life insurance companies
    - Property, casualty, and liability insurance companies
    - Pension funds
    - Banks
    - Credit unions

    The financial institutions for which the liabilities are best matched by an asset mix with a large proportion of long-term assets include

    (1) life insurance companies and banks
    (2) credit unions and property, casualty, and liability insurance companies
    (3) pension funds and life insurance companies
    (4) banks and property, casualty, and liability insurance companies

8. The two major types of investment portfolios held by life insurance companies, known as the general account and the separate account, are very different in terms of their asset mix. However, when the two types of accounts are taken together, the largest asset class industry-wide for insurers' combined general and separate accounts is

    (1) stocks
    (2) bonds
    (3) mortgages
    (4) real estate

9. Fixed-income investments are the most important source of investment income in the life insurance industry.

    (1) True
    (2) False

10. For the life insurance industry as a whole, investment income typically makes up the largest share of total earnings.

    (1) True
    (2) False

11. The most important liabilities of life insurance companies are reserves for obligations to customers.

    (1) True
    (2) False

12. Cash inflows and outflows are one characteristic of assets and liabilities that financial institutions match for purposes of asset-liability management. One example of a cash inflow from investments is

    (1) cash from the sale of financial products
    (2) deposits for retirement contracts
    (3) collection of interest and principal on mortgages
    (4) deposits from asset management clients

Answers to Practice Questions begin on page 93.
Answer choice explanations are available on the CD-ROM on the inside back cover of this book.

CHAPTER 5

Investment Operations in a Financial Services Company

Introduction to Institutional Investing—Chapter Five

Chapter Objectives

After studying this chapter, you should be able to

- Discuss the processes and functions involved in mortgage and real estate operations

- Explain the elements of a mortgage closing

- Discuss the options available for restructuring problem mortgages

- Discuss the uses of an investment information management system

- Explain the functions of a database and identify some commercial databases that are important to institutional investment operations

Outline of Major Topics

Fixed-Income Investment Operations
Equity Investment Operations
Mortgage and Real Estate Investment Operations
    Mortgage Administration
    Mortgage and Real Estate Technical Services
Investment Information Management Systems
    Software for Investment Information Management
    Data Sources for Institutional Investment Operations

Practice Questions

1. In the investment department of a financial services company, the credit research unit typically is associated with equity investment operations.

    (1) True
    (2) False

2. Financial services companies invest in several types of real estate-based investments, such as commercial and residential whole loans. The administration of these loans includes a function known as mortgage underwriting, which refers to the process of

    (1) maintaining the mortgage by collecting payments, keeping records, and sending statements to borrowers
    (2) executing a promissory note and deed of trust in order to transfer the ownership of the property
    (3) completing the administrative tasks necessary to create a mortgage loan
    (4) evaluating the credit of the borrower and the level of risk that the borrower poses to the lender

3. The paragraph below contains two pairs of terms enclosed in parentheses. Determine which term in each pair correctly completes the paragraph. Then select the answer choice containing the two terms that you have chosen.

    For mortgages, the timely payment of principal and interest is referred to as loan (**performance** / **compliance**). Loans that fall behind schedule may be referred to a unit that resolves problem mortgage loans, a process known as asset (**appraisal** / **preservation**).

    (1) performance / appraisal
    (2) performance / preservation
    (3) compliance / appraisal
    (4) compliance / preservation

4. Institutional investment operations typically subscribe to a number of external databases to access market information. Bloomberg is an example of a bond information database.

    (1) True
    (2) False

Answers to Practice Questions begin on page 93.
Answer choice explanations are available on the CD-ROM on the inside back cover of this book.

Financial Reporting for the Investment Function

Introduction to Institutional Investing—Chapter Six

Chapter Objectives

After studying this chapter, you should be able to

- Name and describe four important types of accounting records

- Differentiate among four organizations that set financial reporting standards applicable to investment operations

- Define valuation and describe three standards for asset valuation

- Describe the types of accounting records that investors maintain for their typical investments, including bonds, mortgage investments, stock investments, and real estate

Outline of Major Topics

Types of Accounting Records

Accounting for Invested Assets

Classification of Assets

Asset Valuation

Accounting for Bond Investments

Accounting for Mortgage Investments

Accounting for Stock Investments

Accounting for Real Estate Investments

Investment Income Accounting

Practice Questions

1. For this question, select the answer choice containing the terms that correctly complete the blanks labeled A and B in the statement below.

    Financial services companies in the United States must support several types of financial reporting and must keep different, yet related, sets of accounting records for each of these purposes. Some reports must be prepared according to generally accepted accounting principles (GAAP). GAAP accounting is a type of ___A___ accounting, under which reported asset values are generally based on ___B___.

A	B
(1) solvency-basis	market value
(2) solvency-basis	NAIC ratings
(3) profitability-basis	market value
(4) profitability-basis	NAIC ratings

2. For the purposes of keeping internal accounting records, each company is free to set its own desired accounting standards.

    (1) True
    (2) False

3. One U.S. federal regulatory agency has jurisdiction over all corporations whose stocks or bonds are publicly traded in the United States. This federal agency, which holds the legal authority to set the accounting and reporting methods that public companies use, is known as the

    (1) Internal Revenue Service (IRS)
    (2) Financial Accounting Standards Board (FASB)
    (3) American Institute of Certified Public Accountants (AICPA)
    (4) Securities and Exchange Commission (SEC)

4. Commercial mortgage-backed securities are one type of asset held by financial services companies. In terms of common asset classifications, it is correct to say that commercial mortgage-backed securities are examples of both

    (1) tangible assets and equity investments
    (2) tangible assets and debt securities
    (3) intangible assets and equity investments
    (4) intangible assets and debt securities

5. The paragraph below contains two pairs of terms enclosed in parentheses. Determine which term in each pair correctly completes the paragraph. Then select the answer choice containing the two terms that you have chosen.

   For investment recordkeeping, accountants use several approaches to asset valuation. Under one approach, an asset's historical cost is adjusted for transaction costs, depreciation, amortization, and other amounts. This approach produces what is known as an asset's (**book value** / **fair market value**). If a security is identified as temporarily or permanently impaired, its recorded value will be permanently reduced. This reduction in value is known as a (**discount** / **write-down**).

   (1) book value / discount
   (2) book value / write-down
   (3) fair market value / discount
   (4) fair market value / write-down

6. When a financial institution purchases a bond, the institution typically records the bond's par value in its accounting records, regardless of the amount of the actual purchase price paid for the bond.

   (1) True
   (2) False

7. The Criterion Financial Services Company paid $1,250 for a 10%, $1,000 bond that matures in one year. From the answer choices below, select the response that correctly identifies the bond's effective rate of return and whether Criterion purchased this bond at a discount or at a premium.

	Effective rate of return	Bond purchased at a...
(1)	10%	discount
(2)	8%	discount
(3)	10%	premium
(4)	8%	premium

8. Banner Financial purchased an 8%, $1,000 bond that provides semiannual interest payments. The bond's market value on the date of purchase was $900, and $20 of interest had accrued since the previous interest payment. The purchase price on this bond most likely was

   (1) $920
   (2) $940
   (3) $1,020
   (4) $1,040

9. Insurers in the United States depreciate the cost of real estate over the useful economic life of the property, although land is *not* depreciated.

   (1) True
   (2) False

10. Investment income consists of the earnings a company receives on its invested assets. Earnings from real estate that are classified as investment income include rental income and any gain realized upon the sale of the property at a price higher than the purchase price.

    (1) True
    (2) False

11. Types of investment income include interest income, dividend income, and rental income. One type of investment that produces dividend income, but no interest income or rental income, is

    (1) mortgages
    (2) bonds
    (3) stocks
    (4) policy loans

12. Net investment income is the amount of investment income that remains after deducting expenses and amortization from gross investment income.

    (1) True
    (2) False

Answers to Practice Questions begin on page 93.
Answer choice explanations are available on the CD-ROM on the inside back cover of this book.

CHAPTER 7

Internal and External Investment Reporting

Introduction to Institutional Investing—Chapter Seven

Chapter Objectives

After studying this chapter, you should be able to

- Identify the types of investment activities and events that financial services companies have a duty to report to customers and regulatory agencies

- Discuss the purpose of prospectuses and identify the occasions when financial services companies must provide prospectuses to their customers

- Discuss the required types of reporting financial services companies must accomplish for customer transactions

- Explain the anti-money laundering programs supported by the USA PATRIOT Act and the Bank Secrecy Act and the types of reporting required under those acts

- Discuss the purposes of external and internal reports that companies use to support the goals of asset-liability management

Outline of Major Topics

Reporting Required for Securities
    Routine Reporting to Customers
    Periodic Account Activity Statements
Reporting Taxable Events
Reporting Suspected Money Laundering
Reporting for Asset-Liability Management
    External ALM Reports
    Internal ALM Reports

Practice Questions

1. A prospectus is a written document that describes specific aspects of a security and of the security's issuer, its management, and its financial condition. The following statements are about prospectuses. Three of the statements are true, and one of the statements is false. Select the answer choice containing the **FALSE** statement.

    (1) A prospectus includes information about an investment fund, including its investment objectives, past performance of the fund, fund managers, and fees charged to investors.
    (2) Financial services companies must deliver a revised prospectus to securities owners on an annual basis.
    (3) In the United States, financial services companies must file prospectuses and any revisions of prospectuses with the Internal Revenue Service (IRS).
    (4) Insurance companies are required to provide prospectuses to the purchasers of variable contracts.

2. Financial services companies are subject to certain requirements with regard to routine reporting to customers. In general, the SEC requires that companies mail confirmations of account maintenance transactions to customers within 5 days.

    (1) True
    (2) False

3. In the United States, financial services companies must report to customers and the IRS any account changes that might trigger income, gift, or estate taxes.

    (1) True
    (2) False

4. The following statements are about the USA PATRIOT Act (Patriot Act), a 2001 United States federal law containing anti-money laundering provisions that apply specifically to financial institutions. Select the answer choice containing the correct statement.

    (1) The Patriot Act requires financial institutions to provide customers written notice regarding the manner in which the companies collect and disclose certain types of personal information.
    (2) Under the Patriot Act, financial institutions must file suspicious activity reports (SARs) on any customer transaction that, alone or in the aggregate, involves at least $1,000 in funds or other assets.
    (3) The Securities and Exchange Commission (SEC) is the organization responsible for receiving and following up on suspicious activity reports (SARs) filed by financial institutions.
    (4) The Patriot Act requires that financial institutions establish procedures for verifying the identification of financial account holders.

5. Asset-liability management (ALM) processes establish nontraditional lines of communication that cross the formal boundaries provided within a traditional organizational hierarchy.

    (1) True
    (2) False

6. One report generated by an insurance company's ALM reporting system is the crediting-rate resolution. The crediting-rate resolution typically consists of a

   (1) statement by an appointed actuary that the company's reserves are adequate given the assets supporting them
   (2) description of the company's overall investment growth, broken down by price appreciation and income growth
   (3) formal declaration by the company's board of directors of the rate of interest that the insurer will pay on clients' money held in interest-sensitive products
   (4) comparison of actual investment portfolio yields compared to target investment portfolio yields

7. The paragraph below contains two pairs of terms enclosed in parentheses. Determine which term in each pair correctly completes the paragraph. Then select the answer choice containing the two terms that you have chosen.

   The Ferry Insurance Company generates a number of ALM reports, some of which are developed for internal reporting and others for external reporting. One of the reports generated by Ferry's formal ALM reporting system provides managers with the details of all asset purchases and all dispositions of assets from the portfolio through sales, prepayments (redemptions), or repayment at maturity. This report, which is known as (**an investment activity** / **a duration gap**) report, typically presents yield, term to maturity, duration, and quality rating for each newly acquired asset. Ferry most likely developed this report for (**internal** / **external**) reporting purposes.

   (1) an investment activity / internal
   (2) an investment activity / external
   (3) a duration gap / internal
   (4) a duration gap / external

Answers to Practice Questions begin on page 93.
Answer choice explanations are available on the CD-ROM on the inside back cover of this book.

CHAPTER 8

The Control Function and Ethical Standards in Investments

Introduction to Institutional Investing—Chapter Eight

Chapter Objectives

After studying this chapter, you should be able to

- List and explain several types of unethical and/or illegal practices potentially linked to investment operations

- Describe several principles of internal control that financial services companies use to institute and monitor compliance with ethical standards and legal and regulatory requirements

- Describe the impact of the Sarbanes-Oxley Act on the control function in the United States

- Discuss various types of audits and their purposes

- Describe how government regulators and certain nongovernmental entities support legal and ethical standards and practices in investment operations

Outline of Major Topics

Unethical and Illegal Practices
    Theft and Fraud
    Misuse of Insider Information
    Front Running
    Soft-Dollar Arrangements
    Trading Ahead of Research Reports
    Late Trading and Market Timing Abuses
    Collusion and Intimidation
The Control Function in Investment Operations
    Principles of Internal Control
    Internal Control Provisions of the Sarbanes-Oxley Act
    Auditing
Regulatory Oversight of Investment Operations
Ethical Standards in Investments

Practice Questions

1. Consider the following situations with regard to whether the individuals were involved in insider trading.

    - Saul Hampton, an employee of the Gemini Corporation, communicated material nonpublic information regarding Gemini to his brother, George, and advised him to purchase Gemini's stock. George did not purchase the stock.
    - Based on information that had not been communicated to the general public, Elizabeth Drew, an employee of the Candle Company, advised her friend Cindy Newton, who is not a Candle employee, to purchase Candle stock. Although Ms. Newton purchased the stock, Ms. Drew did not.
    - Carl Brown, an investment professional, sold his stock in the Tellar Company based on his access to an investment analyst's report that was to be released to the general public the following day.

    With regard to these situations, it most likely is correct to say that

    (1) Saul Hampton's actions would not be considered insider trading because George did not act on Saul's advice
    (2) Ms. Drew's actions would not be considered insider trading because she did not benefit directly from the transaction
    (3) Ms. Newton's actions would not be considered insider trading because she was not a Candle employee
    (4) Mr. Brown's actions would not be considered insider trading because the research report was intended for release to the general public
    (5) the actions of all of these individuals would be considered insider trading

2. In securities trading, one prohibited trade practice involves buying or selling a security on the basis of material nonpublic information about a planned block transaction in that security. This practice is known, by definition, as

    (1) late trading
    (2) collusion
    (3) market timing
    (4) front running

3. One example of a soft-dollar arrangement is a situation in which an investment adviser obtains research services from a broker-dealer, and, in exchange, the investment adviser directs client brokerage commissions to the broker-dealer.

    (1) True
    (2) False

4. Fair value pricing is a process by which a financial services company charges a fee equal to a specified percentage of an investor's proceeds if the investor buys and then sells shares within a specified time period.

    (1) True
    (2) False

5. The Regalwood Financial Services Company has implemented a number of internal controls in its investment operations. Among these internal controls is a written policy prohibiting an employee who maintains the accounting records of securities from buying, selling, or otherwise disposing of those securities. This policy illustrates the internal control principle known as

    (1) safeguarding of assets
    (2) segregation of duties
    (3) execution of transactions as authorized
    (4) recording of transactions as executed

6. Using encryption to encode sensitive data is an activity that illustrates the internal control principle known as the physical comparison of recorded amounts.

    (1) True
    (2) False

7. The following statements are about the provisions of the Sarbanes-Oxley Act of 2002, a United States federal law that regulates companies' internal control mechanisms. Three of the statements are true, and one of the statements is false. Select the answer choice containing the **FALSE** statement.

    (1) The Sarbanes-Oxley Act applies only to companies that are publicly traded.
    (2) The Sarbanes-Oxley Act holds management accountable for establishing and maintaining adequate internal control over the company's financial reporting.
    (3) The internal control provisions of the Sarbanes-Oxley Act apply only to internal audits conducted by company staff, not external audits.
    (4) Under the internal control provisions of the Sarbanes-Oxley Act, management's assessment of its internal controls must be supported by a report from the company's auditor.

8. Auditing is an important aspect of a company's internal control function. By definition, one type of audit verifies that a company's operations adhere to applicable laws and regulatory requirements and to the company's policies and procedures. This type of audit is commonly known as a

    (1) compliance audit
    (2) program results audit
    (3) management audit
    (4) performance audit

9. In the United States, the nonprofit organization that is responsible for regulating the over-the-counter securities market is known as the

    (1) Association for Investment Management and Research (AIMR)
    (2) National Association of Insurance Commissioners (NAIC)
    (3) North American Securities Administrators Association (NASAA)
    (4) National Association of Securities Dealers (NASD)

Answers to Practice Questions begin on page 93.
Answer choice explanations are available on the CD-ROM on the inside back cover of this book.

CHAPTER 9

Marketing Investment Services to Institutional Clients

Introduction to Institutional Investing—Chapter Nine

Chapter Objectives

After studying this chapter, you should be able to

- Discuss the benefits institutional clients of financial services companies obtain by outsourcing investment administration

- Explain the challenges of marketing to organizations

- Explain the responsibilities of the investment marketing function of an investment services company

- Identify the selection process an institutional client uses to hire an investment services company

- List the information sought in a typical request for proposal for investment services

- Discuss the topics typically covered in a presentation by an investment services company to a potential institutional client

Outline of Major Topics

Reasons Institutional Clients Purchase Investment Services
Organizational Buying Behavior
Contrast between Institutional Clients and Individual Customers
Organization of the Investment Marketing Function
    Institutional Marketing Operations
    Institutional Product Planning
    Institutional Client Communications
    Institutional Client Service and Relationship Management
    Organizational Units with Sales Responsibilities
Contact with Institutional Clients

New Business Negotiations
  Requests for Proposals
  In-Person Presentations
  Retaining Institutional Clients

Practice Questions

1. The paragraph below contains an incomplete statement. Select the answer choice containing the term that correctly completes the paragraph.

 Marketing investment services to institutional investors requires an understanding of organizational buying behavior. Organizational buying behavior is subject to environmental, organizational, social, and individual influences. An organization's administrative capabilities can best be described as a(n) _____ influence on its organizational buying behavior.

  (1) environmental
  (2) organizational
  (3) social
  (4) individual

2. Investment services providers face different challenges in marketing to institutional buyers than in marketing financial services to individual buyers. One factor that contributes to differences in the marketing approaches used with these two types of buyers is that

  (1) organizational purchasing decisions typically employ a less complex process than do purchase decisions by individuals
  (2) marketing financial services to organizations does not require the use of personal selling approaches, whereas marketing financial services to individuals relies heavily on personal selling
  (3) organizations tend to adopt a less formal approach to large purchase decisions than do individual buyers
  (4) organizational buyers typically have more opportunity to negotiate with the seller for features, services, and pricing than do individual buyers

3. The institutional marketing department of a financial services company supports a number of functions related to the marketing of investment services to institutional clients. Assume that an institutional marketing department includes a client communications unit, a product planning unit, a consultant relations unit, and an institutional client services unit. Of these functional units, the one that most likely is responsible for the preparation of proposals in response to requests for proposals (RFPs) from potential clients is the

  (1) client communications unit
  (2) product planning unit
  (3) consultant relations unit
  (4) institutional client services unit

Answers to Practice Questions begin on page 93.
Answer choice explanations are available on the CD-ROM on the inside back cover of this book.

Answers to
Practice Questions

Answers to Practice Questions

Introduction to Institutional Investing—Chapter 1

1. p. 7...1
2. p. 7...2
3. p. 10...4
4. p. 11...1
5. pp. 13–14.......................................2
6. pp. 15–16.......................................4
7. p. 17...3
8. pp. 19–20.......................................4
9. p. 19...2

Introduction to Institutional Investing—Chapter 2

1. pp. 29–30.......................................1
2. p. 30...2
3. p. 32...1
4. pp. 34–35.......................................2
5. p. 36...2
6. p. 36...3
7. p. 37...4
8. pp. 37, 38.......................................4
9. p. 38...2
10. pp. 41–43.......................................4
11. p. 45...1
12. pp. 47–48.......................................1

Introduction to Institutional Investing—Chapter 3

1. pp. 66, 67.......................................1
2. p. 68...1
3. pp. 69, 72.......................................2
4. pp. 70–71.......................................2
5. pp. 74–75.......................................3
6. p. 78...1

Introduction to Institutional Investing—Chapter 4

1. pp. 87–88.......................................3
2. p. 88...2
3. p. 89...4
4. p. 91...3
5. pp. 93, 97.......................................3
6. pp. 94-95 1

7. pp. 95–96.......................................3
8. pp. 97, 98.......................................2
9. p. 100...1
10. p. 101...2
11. p. 102...1
12. p. 103...3

Introduction to Institutional Investing—Chapter 5

1. pp. 112, 114...................................2
2. p. 117...4
3. p. 119...2
4. p. 124...1

Introduction to Institutional Investing—Chapter 6

1. p. 134...3
2. p. 135...1
3. p. 136...4
4. pp. 139, 146...................................4
5. p. 141...2
6. p. 142...2
7. pp. 142, 144...................................4
8. pp. 145–146...................................1
9. p. 148...1
10. pp. 148–149...................................2
11. pp. 148–149...................................3
12. p. 150...1

Introduction to Institutional Investing—Chapter 7

1. pp. 164–165...................................3
2. pp. 166–167...................................2
3. p. 168...1
4. pp. 169–171...................................4
5. p. 172...1
6. p. 174...3
7. pp. 175–177...................................1

Sample
Examination

This examination contains 75 objective questions. Each question is valued at 1.3333 points. For each question, circle the number of your chosen response.

1. One type of mutual fund actively and directly incorporates ethics and morality into the investment decision. This type of mutual fund is known, by definition, as a

   (1) socially responsible fund
   (2) sector fund
   (3) value fund
   (4) money market fund

2. The Elfstone Corporation issued bonds by means of a private placement. This information indicates that Elfstone

   (1) sold its bonds in the money market rather than in the capital market
   (2) was required to register these bonds with the Securities and Exchange Commission (SEC) before it sold them
   (3) sold its bonds directly to one or more qualified investors
   (4) hired an investment banker to sell its bonds

3. Assets can be classified according to whether they are short-term (current) assets or long-term (noncurrent) assets and according to whether they are debt securities or equity investments. A 15-year bond that an insurer plans to hold until maturity is an example of both a

   (1) short-term asset and a debt security
   (2) short-term asset and an equity investment
   (3) long-term asset and a debt security
   (4) long-term asset and an equity investment

4. In financial services companies, mortgage administration includes a number of functions. One of these functions refers to the process of creating a mortgage loan. By definition, this process is known as

   (1) mortgage underwriting
   (2) mortgage origination
   (3) mortgage servicing
   (4) mortgage closing

5. One popular measure of risk is known as beta. One true statement about beta is

   (1) that it measures the diversifiable risk of a security
   (2) that the beta for the market is set at "0.00"
   (3) that, the higher a stock's beta, the smaller should be its level of expected return
   (4) that nearly all stocks have positive betas

6. In financial services companies, one type of investment professional is responsible for executing purchases and sales of publicly traded securities. By definition, this type of investment professional is known as

    (1) an investment analyst
    (2) an asset trader
    (3) a portfolio manager
    (4) an investment accountant

7. The paragraph below contains an incomplete statement. Select the answer choice containing the term that correctly completes the paragraph.

    Securities laws protect investors and participants in the financial marketplace. The most important securities laws are those enacted by the federal government. For example, as a result of the _____, brokers have been able to charge whatever brokerage commissions they deem appropriate.

    (1) Securities Acts Amendments of 1975
    (2) Maloney Act of 1938
    (3) Investment Advisers Act of 1940
    (4) Fair Disclosure Rule, or Regulation FD

8. For this question, if statements (1) through (3) are all correct, select answer choice (4). Otherwise, select the one correct statement.

    Three commonly cited theories that are used to explain the term structure of interest rates are the expectations hypothesis, the liquidity preference theory, and the market segmentation theory. The following statement(s) can correctly be made about these theories:

    (1) According to the expectations hypothesis, a decreasing inflation expectation results in an upward-sloping yield curve, whereas an increasing inflation expectation results in a downward-sloping yield curve.
    (2) The liquidity preference theory states that, intuitively, long-term bond rates should be higher than short-term rates because of the added risks involved with the longer maturities.
    (3) According to the market segmentation theory, low interest rates in the short-term segment of the market and high interest rates in the long-term segment of the market cause a downward-sloping yield curve.
    (4) All of the above statements are correct.

9. Bonds and notes issued by the U.S. Treasury are a dominant force in the fixed-income market. One characteristic of Treasury *bonds* is that they generally

    (1) carry 10-year maturities
    (2) are exempt from state and federal income taxes
    (3) are sold in $1,000 denominations
    (4) are traded solely in U.S. securities markets

10. One basic theory of the behavior of efficient markets is known as the efficient markets hypothesis (EMH). One tenet of the EMH is that

    (1) information on events that impact the stock market tends to be disseminated at evenly spaced intervals
    (2) one individual investor, acting alone, has the potential to affect the prices of securities
    (3) investors often act erroneously to new information, causing swings in securities prices that are highly unpredictable
    (4) information is widely available to all investors at approximately the same time, and this information is practically "free," or nearly so

11. Portfolios can be grouped according to their investment styles. Four common portfolio styles are:

    • Growth portfolios
    • Index portfolios
    • Income portfolios
    • Value portfolios

    In a life insurance company, the portfolios that support fixed life insurance and fixed annuity products are typically

    (1) growth portfolios
    (2) index portfolios
    (3) income portfolios
    (4) value portfolios

12. Chang Lee used the dividend valuation model (DVM) known as the constant growth model to price the common stock of the Gardenia Corporation. Gardenia stock currently pays dividends of $2.00 a share. In addition, Mr. Lee estimated that dividends are growing at a rate of 8% per year and that investing in Gardenia stock should provide a required return of 12%. Applying the constant growth dividend model, Mr. Lee determined that, in order to receive the required return of 12% on this investment, he should pay for Gardenia stock no more than

    (1) $18 per share
    (2) $25 per share
    (3) $50 per share
    (4) $54 per share

13. The paragraph below contains two pairs of terms enclosed in parentheses. Determine which term in each pair correctly completes the paragraph. Then select the answer choice containing the two terms that you have chosen.

Conditions in the securities markets are commonly classified as "bull" or "bear," depending on the direction in which securities prices are moving. (**Bull** / **Bear**) markets are unfavorable markets normally associated with falling prices, investor pessimism, economic slowdown, and government restraint. In general, investors experience higher, or positive, returns on common stock investments during a (**bull** / **bear**) market.

    (1) Bull / bull
    (2) Bull / bear
    (3) Bear / bull
    (4) Bear / bear

14. Julian Nestor, an employee of the Triangle Corporation, purchased shares of Triangle's stock while he was in possession of material nonpublic information about Triangle. Mr. Nestor also communicated this material nonpublic information to his neighbor, Maria Sanchez, who then also purchased shares of Triangle's stock. In this situation, insider trading was most likely committed by

    (1) both Mr. Nestor and Ms. Sanchez
    (2) Mr. Nestor only
    (3) Ms. Sanchez only
    (4) neither Mr. Nestor nor Ms. Sanchez

15. The three basic risk preferences for investors are the risk-indifferent investor, the risk-averse investor, and the risk-seeking investor. The following statements are about these types of risk preferences. Select the answer choice containing the correct statement.

    (1) Most investors are risk seeking.
    (2) The risk-averse investor requires a decrease in return for a given risk increase.
    (3) A risk-indifferent investor does not require a change in return as compensation for greater risk.
    (4) The risk-seeking investor requires greater return in exchange for greater risk.

Use the following information to answer questions 16 through 23.

Cassandra Maxwell was considering investing in the common stock of the Vector Corporation. Before making a decision to purchase Vector's stock, however, Ms. Maxwell researched the company. The results of her research indicated that Vector has a market capitalization of $2 billion, solid fundamentals, very little debt, and a long history of steady profit growth. Although Vector stock pays only a modest level of dividends, the stock is considered ideal for investors seeking quality long-term growth. As part of her research, Ms. Maxwell perused a detailed report that contained the following information on Vector:

- **Information A** detailed Vector's insider decisions in the past 12 months
- **Information B** described Vector's capital structure for the past 10 years
- **Information C** outlined the monthly price ranges for Vector's stock for the past 5 years
- **Information D** indicated that the beta for Vector's common stock was currently +1.5 and that this beta is expected to hold for the next 3 years

Next Ms. Maxwell used the capital asset pricing model (CAPM) to determine the required return on Vector Stock. Ms. Maxwell's sources indicated a risk-free rate of return of 6%, a market return of 10%, and an expected inflation premium of 3%. Ms. Maxwell also used the stock valuation model known as the dividends-and-earnings (D&E) approach to calculate a market price of $60 per share for Vector's common stock. Vector's current market price is $62 per share.

As a result of her research, Ms. Maxwell decided to purchase the Vector stock. She then contacted her broker by calling a toll-free telephone number and placed an order to buy 80 shares of Vector stock when the price of the stock falls to $60 or less. Although Ms. Maxwell's broker charges low commission fees to make transactions for his customers, he is not a deep-discount broker. He also provides no free research information or investment advice to his customers.

16. This information indicates that Vector's stock is most likely a type of

    (1) small-cap stock known as a new-economy stock
    (2) small-cap stock known as a baby blue chip
    (3) mid-cap stock known as a new-economy stock
    (4) mid-cap stock known as a baby blue chip

17. Investment information can be categorized as either descriptive or analytical. Of the four examples of information about Vector listed above, the one that is an example of *analytical* information is

    (1) Information A
    (2) Information B
    (3) Information C
    (4) Information D

18. According to the CAPM, the required return on Vector stock is equal to

   (1) 6%
   (2) 9%
   (3) 12%
   (4) 13%

19. This information indicates that the real rate of return at this time is equal to

   (1) 3%
   (2) 4%
   (3) 7%
   (4) 9%

20. In using the dividends-and-earnings (D&E) approach to calculate the value of Vector's stock, Ms. Maxwell most likely used a formula in which the

   (1) price of a share of Vector's stock was equal to Vector's return on equity (ROE) multiplied by Vector's retention rate, or "rr"
   (2) price of a share of Vector's stock was equal to Vector's earnings per share (EPS) divided by Vector's price/earnings (P/E) ratio
   (3) price of a share of Vector's stock was equal to the annual dividends on the stock divided by the required rate of return for Vector's stock
   (4) present value of a share of Vector's stock was equal to the present value of the future dividends of the stock added to the present value of the projected price of the Vector stock at the date when Ms. Maxwell plans to sell it

21. Two types of analysis used to evaluate investments are fundamental analysis and security analysis. In deciding to purchase Vector stock, Ms. Maxwell used

   (1) both fundamental analysis and security analysis
   (2) fundamental analysis, but not security analysis
   (3) security analysis, but not fundamental analysis
   (4) neither fundamental analysis nor security analysis

22. With respect to the type of order and the type of transaction illustrated by this situation, it is most likely correct to say that this situation illustrates a type of order known as a

   (1) limit order and a type of transaction known as an odd-lot transaction
   (2) limit order and a type of transaction known as a round-lot transaction
   (3) market order and a type of transaction known as an odd-lot transaction
   (4) market order and a type of transaction known as a round-lot transaction

23. The type of broker that Ms. Maxwell contacted to execute her order to purchase Vector stock is most likely known as

   (1) a full-service broker
   (2) a discount broker
   (3) an electronic broker
   (4) an online broker

24. The cost of investing in an open-end mutual fund depends on the types of fees and load charges that the fund levies on investors. One type of fee is levied annually by some mutual funds to cover management and other operating costs. This fee, which can amount to as much as 1% of the average net assets, is known as a

    (1) redemption fee
    (2) front-end load
    (3) back-end load
    (4) 12(b)-1 fee

25. In one type of bond swap, the investor replaces a bond that has a capital loss for a similar security. This type of swap is used to offset a gain generated in another part of the investor's portfolio. From the answer choices below, select the response that correctly indicates whether this type of bond swap is known as a yield pickup swap or a tax swap and whether the Internal Revenue Service (IRS) allows investors to use identical issues in these swap transactions.

Type of Bond Swap	Identical Issues Allowed?
(1) yield pickup swap	yes
(2) yield pickup swap	no
(3) tax swap	yes
(4) tax swap	no

26. Financial tables include various interest factors that simplify time value calculations. Two of these tables present the Future-Value Interest Factors for One Dollar (*FVIF*) and the Present-Value Interest Factors for One Dollar (*PVIF*). The following statements are about these *FVIF*s and *PVIF*s. Select the answer choice containing the correct statement.

    (1) For a given interest rate, the future value of a dollar increases with the passage of time.
    (2) As the interest rate increases for any given year, the future-value interest factor decreases.
    (3) The present-value interest factor for a single sum is always greater than 1.
    (4) The higher the discount rate for a given year, the greater the present-value interest factor.

27. The paragraph below contains two pairs of terms enclosed in parentheses. Determine which term in each pair correctly completes the paragraph. Then select the answer choice containing the two terms that you have chosen.

Government, business, and individuals are the three key participants in the investment process. Each may act as a supplier and a demander of funds. In general, businesses are net (**suppliers / demanders**) of funds, and individuals as a group are net (**suppliers / demanders**) of funds.

    (1) suppliers / suppliers
    (2) suppliers / demanders
    (3) demanders / suppliers
    (4) demanders / demanders

28. The following statement(s) can correctly be made about insurers' investments in mortgages:

    A. Because mortgages are a type of fixed-income security, they are a good match for the general account portfolios of insurance companies.

    B. The greatest share of mortgages held by insurers is in commercial mortgages and commercial mortgage-backed securities (CMBSs).

     (1) Both A and B
     (2) A only
     (3) B only
     (4) Neither A nor B

29. Jocelyn Picard wants to select the less risky of two alternative investments—X and Y. The following information applies to these two investments:

	Investment X	Investment Y
Average Return	10%	15%
Standard Deviation	8%	9%

From the answer choices below, select the response that correctly indicates the coefficient of variation for Investment X and the coefficient of variation for Investment Y and which of the two investments would be considered less risky.

	Coefficient of Variation for Investment X	Coefficient of Variation for Investment Y	Less Risky Investment
(1)	0.80	0.60	Investment X
(2)	0.80	0.60	Investment Y
(3)	1.25	1.67	Investment X
(4)	1.25	1.67	Investment Y

30. Financial services companies in the United States must support several types of financial reporting and must keep different, yet related, sets of accounting records for each of these purposes. One of these types of accounting records supports financial reporting to investors and the public. These records focus on showing the company's financial stability along with its profitability. By definition, these types of accounting records are known as

     (1) management accounting records
     (2) statutory accounting records
     (3) generally accepted accounting principles (GAAP) accounting records
     (4) internal accounting records

31. Use the following information about the Purple Corporation to answer this question:

> Total assets $10,000,000
> Total liabilities .... $ 3,000,000
> Number of shares of common stock outstanding 100,000
> Current market price of common stock .... $80 per share
> Par value of common stock .... $1 per share

Purple has never issued preferred stock. This information indicates that Purple's book value is equal to

    (1) $5,000,000
    (2) $7,000,000
    (3) $8,000,000
    (4) $15,000,000

32. The Wisteria Fund is a type of investment company that operates with a fixed number of shares outstanding, and it does not issue new shares of stock. Shares in Wisteria are actively traded in the secondary market, and all trading takes place between investors in the open market, with Wisteria playing no role in either buy or sell transactions. The share prices for Wisteria are determined not only by their net asset values (NAVs) but also by general supply and demand conditions in the stock market. This information indicates that Wisteria is a type of investment company known as

    (1) a unit investment trust
    (2) an exchange-traded fund (ETF)
    (3) a closed-end investment company
    (4) an open-end investment company

33. Companies may pay dividends in the form of either cash dividends or stock dividends. The following statements are about cash dividends and stock dividends. Select the answer choice containing the correct statement.

    (1) In general, stockholders like to see cash dividend payout ratios of more than 60%.
    (2) In general, cash dividends tend to increase over time, as companies' earnings grow.
    (3) The market value of an investor's shareholdings after a stock dividend is likely to be more than it was before the stock dividend.
    (4) With both cash dividends and stock dividends, the dividends are not taxed until the stocks are actually sold.

34. The following information provides the ratings given to four different bonds by Moody's and Standard & Poor's (S&P):

	Moody's	S&P
Bond 1	Baa	BBB
Bond 2	Ca	CC
Bond 3	Aa	A
Bond 4	Ba	BB

This information indicates that

(1) Bond 1 is a junk bond
(2) Bond 2 has the highest exposure to market risk
(3) Bond 3 has a split rating
(4) Bond 4 is an investment-grade bond

35. Sebastian Turner, an individual investor, focuses on the stocks of companies that are out of favor with the market for some reason. Stock prices for these companies are low compared to their fundamentals: These stocks have lower price/earnings (P/E) ratios, lower price-to-book ratios, and higher dividend yields than the rest of the market. In seeking out the stocks of these companies, Mr. Turner generally uses a buy-and-hold strategy. This information indicates that Mr. Turner's investment style is known as

(1) growth investing
(2) value investing
(3) momentum investing
(4) sector rotation

36. The risk associated with a given investment vehicle may result from a combination of possible sources. One type of risk refers to the chance that inflation or deflation will adversely affect investment returns. This type of risk is known, by definition, as

(1) purchasing power risk
(2) financial risk
(3) liquidity risk
(4) business risk

37. Two dispute resolution processes that can be used to resolve disputes between investors and brokers are mediation and arbitration. The following statement(s) can correctly be made about mediation and arbitration:

A. In mediation, the mediator does not impose a solution on the parties to the dispute.
B. Many brokerage firms require customers to resolve disputes through binding arbitration.

(1) Both A and B
(2) A only
(3) B only
(4) Neither A nor B

38. In deciding which securities are most appropriate for a particular situation, an investor needs to consider such issue characteristics as availability, safety, liquidity, and yield. Consider the following four types of short-term investment vehicles:

    - A U.S. Treasury bill (91-day)
    - An asset management account
    - A negotiated order of withdrawal (NOW) account
    - A money market deposit account (MMDA)

    Of these types of short-term investment vehicles, the one that generally has the highest

    (1) *availability* is the NOW account
    (2) *safety* is the asset management account
    (3) *liquidity* is the U.S. Treasury bill
    (4) *yield* is the MMDA

39. On Thursday, May 1, the board of directors of the Tuxedo Corporation declared a quarterly stock dividend of 50 cents per share to holders of record on Friday, May 16. Checks will be mailed to holders of record on Friday, May 30. In this situation, the ex-dividend date is most likely

    (1) May 1
    (2) May 13
    (3) May 16
    (4) May 27

40. The paragraph below contains two pairs of terms enclosed in parentheses. Determine which term in each pair correctly completes the paragraph. Then select the answer choice containing the two terms that you have chosen.

    Portfolio management strategies can be classified according to whether they are active or passive. (**Active / Passive**) portfolio management is a style or strategy that relies upon careful portfolio construction and infrequent trading. Of these two portfolio investment strategies, (**active / passive**) portfolio management typically has lower trading volume and staff costs.

    (1) Active / active
    (2) Active / passive
    (3) Passive / active
    (4) Passive / passive

Use the following information extracted from the Tanglewood Corporation's 2003 year-end financial statements to answer questions 41 through 43.

Current Assets..$800,000
Total Assets...$4,000,000
Current Liabilities...$500,000
Total Liabilities..$2,000,000
Annual Sales...$6,000,000
Inventory..$500,000
Market Price for Tanglewood Common Stock $60
Earnings Per Share for Tanglewood Common Stock $2
Dividends Per Share of Tanglewood Common Stock.................. $0.15

41. This information indicates that Tanglewood's net working capital for 2003 was equal to

    (1) 1.60
    (2) 2.00
    (3) $300,000
    (4) $2,000,000

42. This information indicates that Tanglewood's total asset turnover for 2003 was equal to

    (1) 0.125
    (2) 0.67
    (3) 1.5
    (4) 12

43. This information indicates that, assuming a 3- to 5-year growth rate in earnings of 15%, Tanglewood's PEG ratio for 2003 was equal to

    (1) 0.0025
    (2) 0.075
    (3) 0.50
    (4) 2.00

*   *   *   *   *   *

44. Investors employing economic analysis can track the behavior of the economy through the business cycle, which reflects changes in total economic activity over time. One widely followed measure of the business cycle estimates the total dollar value of all goods and services produced in a country over a time period of one year. By definition, this measure is known as

    (1) industrial production
    (2) gross domestic product (GDP)
    (3) the index of leading indicators
    (4) the relative strength index (RSI)

45. One type of bond is a PIK-bond, or payment-in-kind bond. A PIK-bond can correctly be defined as a

   (1) mortgage-backed bond whose holders are divided into classes based on the length of investment desired
   (2) type of bond that makes monthly payments in the form of both interest and principal
   (3) type of pass-through debt security backed by pools of auto loans and credit card bills
   (4) type of high-risk bond in which the issuer has the right to make annual interest payments in new bonds rather than in cash

46. Life insurance companies have two different major types of investment portfolios—the general account and separate accounts. From the answer choices below, select the response that correctly indicates, industry-wide, the largest asset class for insurers' general accounts and the largest asset class for insurers' separate accounts.

Largest Asset Class for Insurers' General Accounts	Largest Asset Class for Insurers' Separate Accounts
(1) bonds	stocks
(2) stocks	bonds
(3) mortgages	bonds
(4) stocks	stocks

47. Company A and Company B are two relatively new companies, both of which provide networking systems and online services to businesses. Company A has a higher burn rate than Company B. This information indicates that Company A is

   (1) earning a reinvestment rate on its investments that is significantly lower than what Company B is earning
   (2) using up its supply of cash over time more quickly than is Company B
   (3) using more equity and less debt to finance its business than is Company B
   (4) receiving lower returns on its high-risk investments than is Company B

48. A single bond issuer can have a number of different bonds outstanding at any given point in time. For example, bond issues can be classified as either junior or senior. One example of a *junior* bond is

   (1) an equipment trust certificate
   (2) an income bond
   (3) a first and refunding bond
   (4) a collateral trust bond

49. In investments terminology, illegal activities are represented by

   A. Pyramiding
   B. Churning
   C. Late trading
   D. Short selling

      (1) A, B, C, and D
      (2) A, B, and D only
      (3) B, C, and D only
      (4) B and C only
      (5) C only

50. For this question, if statements (1) through (3) are all correct, select answer choice (4). Otherwise, select the one correct statement.

Three types of financial statements are used in company analysis: the balance sheet, the income statement, and the statement of cash flows. The following statement(s) can correctly be made about these types of financial statements:

   (1) The balance sheet is a financial summary of the operating results of a firm covering a specified period of time, usually one year.
   (2) The income statement is a financial summary of a firm's assets, liabilities, and owners' equity at a single point in time.
   (3) The statement of cash flows provides a financial summary of a firm's cash flow and other events that caused changes in the firm's cash position.
   (4) All of the above statements are correct.

51. Types of mutual funds include the following:

   • Growth funds
   • Bond funds
   • Aggressive growth funds
   • Growth-and-income funds

Of these types of mutual funds, income is the primary investment objective of

   (1) growth funds
   (2) bond funds
   (3) aggressive growth funds
   (4) growth-and-income funds

52. In one type of investment income allocation method used by insurers, the insurer assigns investment income to each of its product lines in proportion to the reserves attributable to that product line. For example, if 40% of an insurer's reserves are for group life insurance, then the organizational unit that is accountable for group life insurance is allocated 40% of the insurer's investment income. By definition, this type of investment income allocation method is known as the

    (1) investment segmentation method
    (2) mean liabilities method
    (3) investment year method
    (4) modified Dietz method

53. Denise Chung established a margin account with her broker. Ms. Chung then purchased 100 shares of the stock of the Butterfly Corporation for $60 per share at a time when the initial margin requirement was 60%. At the time of purchase, Ms. Chung put up the minimum amount of funds and financed the remainder of the purchase price by using a margin loan. From the answer choices below, select the response that correctly indicates the debit balance in Ms. Chung's account and whether Ms. Chung's account would become restricted if the market price of Butterfly stock falls to $50 per share.

Debit Balance in Account	Account Restricted?
(1) $2,400	Yes
(2) $2,400	No
(3) $3,600	Yes
(4) $3,600	No

54. When dealing with investment horizons of more than one year, sophisticated investors generally use a measure known as yield, or the internal rate of return. The internal rate of return can correctly be defined as the

    (1) annual rate of return earned by a long-term investment, using simple interest only
    (2) discount rate that produces a present value of the investment's benefits that just equals the investment's cost
    (3) rate of return earned on interest or other income received from an investment over its investment horizon
    (4) compound annual rate of change in the value of a stream of income

55. Types of securities markets include the over-the-counter (OTC) market and the alternative trading systems known as the third market and the fourth market. With respect to whether dealers participate in the OTC market, the third market, and the fourth market, it is most likely correct to say that dealers participate in

    (1) all of these kinds of markets
    (2) the OTC market and the third market, but not in the fourth market
    (3) the OTC market and the fourth market, but not in the third market
    (4) the OTC market, but not in the third market or the fourth market

56. The paragraph below contains two pairs of terms enclosed in parentheses. Determine which term in each pair correctly completes the paragraph. Then select the answer choice containing the two terms that you have chosen.

Two types of financial ratios are leverage ratios and profitability ratios. One example of a leverage ratio is (**accounts receivable turnover** / **times interest earned**). One profitability ratio, known as net profit margin, can correctly be calculated by dividing a firm's net profit after taxes by its (**total assets** / **total revenues**).

    (1) accounts receivable turnover / total assets
    (2) accounts receivable turnover / total revenues
    (3) times interest earned / total assets
    (4) times interest earned / total revenues

57. One approach to asset allocation used by institutional portfolio managers is a form of market timing that uses stock-index futures and bond futures to change a portfolio's asset allocation. This approach to asset allocation is known, by definition, as

    (1) tactical asset allocation
    (2) the flexible-weightings approach
    (3) the fixed-weightings approach
    (4) the asset allocation fund approach

58. The following statements are about characteristics of margin trading. Select the answer choice containing the correct statement.

    (1) The minimum initial margin requirement established by the Federal Reserve Board is the same for all types of securities that can be margined.
    (2) In calculating the return on invested capital from a margin transaction, the investor is concerned with the rate of return earned on only the portion of the funds that he or she provided.
    (3) When a margin account becomes restricted, the investor is required to put up additional cash or equity to bring the equity back up to the initial margin.
    (4) The official maintenance margin on Treasury bonds is currently set by the Federal Reserve Board at 25%.

Use the following information to answer questions 59 through 61.

In 2000, Heidi Zimmerman paid $930 to purchase from the Heliotrope Corporation a $1,000 par value bond with a 9% coupon. The bond contains a feature which states that Heliotrope is prohibited, under any circumstances, from retiring the bond prior to its maturity. The current market price of this bond is $900.

59. One true statement about this situation is

   (1) that this bond sold at a premium when Ms. Zimmerman purchased it in 2000
   (2) that this bond obligates Heliotrope to pay Ms. Zimmerman exactly $930 at its maturity
   (3) that, when Ms. Zimmerman purchased this bond in 2000, market interest rates were greater than 9%
   (4) that current market interest rates are lower than 9%

60. The feature in this bond which states that Heliotrope is prohibited, under any circumstances, from retiring the bond prior to its maturity is known, by definition, as

   (1) a call feature
   (2) a refunding feature
   (3) a sinking fund feature
   (4) an immunization feature

61. The current yield on this bond is

   (1) 8.1%
   (2) 9.3%
   (3) 9.7%
   (4) 10.0%

*　*　*　*　*　*

62. Mortgages can be classified according to quality as follows:

   • Mortgages in good standing
   • Restructured mortgages
   • Overdue mortgages
   • Mortgages in process of foreclosure
   • Foreclosed property

   The vast majority of the mortgages held in life insurance company portfolios can be classified as

   (1) mortgages in good standing
   (2) restructured mortgages
   (3) overdue mortgages
   (4) mortgages in process of foreclosure

63. Asset-liability management (ALM) reports can be classified according to whether they are developed for internal reporting or external reporting. One example of an ALM report that insurers develop for *external* reporting is

   (1) a duration gap report
   (2) an actuarial opinion and memorandum (AOM)
   (3) an investment activity report
   (4) an investment portfolio performance review

64. Technical analysis deals with the behavior of the stock market itself and the various economic forces at work in the marketplace. A number of tools, or technical indicators, can be used to assess the state of the marketplace. One widely followed technical indicator is known as the theory of contrary opinion. The theory of contrary opinion states that

   (1) the amount and type of odd-lot trading is an indicator of the current state of the market and pending changes
   (2) the market is considered strong when volume rises during a decline or drops off during a rising market
   (3) the market is considered strong so long as the number of stocks that increase on a given day exceeds the number of stocks that decline on that day
   (4) a significant shift upward in short interest is believed to indicate optimism concerning the current state of the market, even though it may signal pessimism with regard to future levels of market demand

65. Yield spreads, or interest rate differentials, exist among the various market sectors for bonds. The following statements are about these market yields and yield spreads. Select the answer choice containing the correct statement.

   (1) There is generally an inverse relationship between the coupon an issue carries and its yield.
   (2) Bonds that are freely callable generally provide lower returns, at least at date of issue, than do bonds that are noncallable.
   (3) In the taxable sector, Treasury bonds have the lowest yields, whereas corporates have the highest yields.
   (4) In the municipal sector, general obligation bonds yield more than revenue bonds.

66. Investment income consists of the earnings a company receives on its invested assets. Types of investment income include interest income, dividend income, and rental income. One type of investment that produces rental income, but no interest income or dividend income, is

   (1) stocks
   (2) bonds
   (3) real estate
   (4) mortgages

67. The coefficient of determination—R^2—can be used to evaluate a beta coefficient statistically. In general, a well-diversified stock portfolio will have a beta equation R^2 of

 (1) exactly 0.00
 (2) from 0.20 to 0.50
 (3) around 0.90
 (4) exactly 1.00

68. Financial services organizations follow certain principles in developing and implementing an internal control system. From the answer choices below, select the response that *best* describes, for a financial services company known as the Transitive Corporation, an example of the internal control principle known as the *safeguarding of assets*.

 (1) Every quarter, Transitive's investment staff reconciles its internally generated inventory of investments against information provided to it by third parties.
 (2) All new stock traders at Transitive are required to obtain authorization for all stock purchases or sales in excess of $20,000, whereas more experienced stock traders at Transitive are required to obtain authorization for all stock purchases or sales in excess of $50,000.
 (3) Transitive records all completed transactions in the correct accounting period, in the correct accounts, in the correct physical units, and in the correct monetary amounts.
 (4) Transitive places the certificates for its securities in the custody of a third party so that Transitive can maintain control of its securities without having to physically handle the certificates for those securities.

69. Series EE savings bonds are the well-known savings bonds that have been available for decades. One characteristic of Series EE savings bonds is that they generally

 (1) are issued in denominations of $1,000 only
 (2) are exempt from state and local taxes
 (3) pay interest periodically over the life of the bonds
 (4) have specified maturities of 6 months to 5 years

70. In the United States, one federal law contains anti-money laundering provisions that require financial institutions to take specified actions. These actions include verifying the identification of financial account holders, establishing internal anti-money laundering programs that meet specified minimum standards, cooperating with other financial institutions to deter customers from engaging in money laundering activities, and reporting suspected money laundering transactions by customers. This federal law is known as the

 (1) Gramm-Leach-Bliley (GLB) Act
 (2) Sarbanes-Oxley Act
 (3) USA PATRIOT Act
 (4) Financial Guaranty Insurance Company (FGIC) Act

71. The financial statements of the Yoyo-Dyne Corporation indicate that the company has treasury stock. This information indicates that Yoyo-Dyne

    (1) repurchased previously issued shares of its own stock
    (2) converted one of its subsidiaries to a stand-alone company by distributing stock in that new company to existing shareholders
    (3) issued its common stock in different classes, each of which offers different privileges and benefits to its holders
    (4) increased the number of shares of its common stock outstanding by exchanging a specified number of new shares of stock for each outstanding share

72. Bond duration is a measure of bond price volatility, which captures both price and reinvestment risks and which is used to indicate how a bond will react in different interest rate environments. The following statements can correctly be made about bond duration. Select the answer choice containing the correct statement.

    (1) The duration of a bond is fixed and does not change over time.
    (2) A bond's duration and volatility are inversely related, which means that the shorter the duration, the more volatility there is in bond prices, and vice versa.
    (3) The concept of bond duration considers maturity alone to be a sufficient measure of the time dimension of bonds.
    (4) For all bonds other than zero-coupon bonds, duration measures are always less than their actual maturities.

73. Natalie Fox is considering investing her excess funds in a savings instrument in which the funds must remain on deposit for five years. Should Ms. Fox withdraw any of the funds prior to the end of the five-year period, she will incur an interest penalty. On the positive side, this investment offers Ms. Fox a highly competitive return, along with federal insurance protection of up to $100,000 per deposit. This information indicates that Ms. Fox is considering investing in a

    (1) certificate of deposit (CD)
    (2) NOW (negotiated order of withdrawal) account
    (3) money market deposit account (MMDA)
    (4) passbook savings account

74. In the United States, organized securities exchanges include the New York Stock Exchange (NYSE), the American Stock Exchange (AMEX), regional stock exchanges, and options and futures exchanges. The following statements are about these organized securities exchanges. Three of the statements are true, and one of the statements is false. Select the answer choice containing the **FALSE** statement.

    (1) Of the organized U.S. stock exchanges, the greatest annual dollar volume of shares is traded on the NYSE.
    (2) In terms of dollar volume of trading, the AMEX is actually smaller than the two largest regional exchanges—the Chicago and the Pacific.
    (3) The majority of securities listed on regional exchanges are also listed on the NYSE or the AMEX.
    (4) The only exchange for trading options and futures is the Chicago Board of Trade (CBT).

75. Investors tend to follow different investment philosophies as they move through different stages of the life cycle. The following statements are about investing over the life cycle. Three of the statements are true, and one of the statements is false. Select the answer choice containing the **FALSE** statement.

   (1) For investors approaching their retirement years, preservation of capital and current income become the principal investment concerns.

   (2) Most young investors, in their twenties and thirties, tend to prefer growth-oriented investments that stress capital gains rather than current income.

   (3) For investors over the age of 60, typical investments are low-risk common stocks, high-yielding government bonds, quality corporate bonds, and bank certificates of deposit (CDs).

   (4) Investors approaching the middle-age consolidation stage of life tend to favor speculative vehicles, such as high-risk common stocks, options, and futures.

END OF EXAMINATION

Text References
and Answers to
Sample Examination

Text References and Answers to Sample Examination

Interactive Study Aid Software Instructions

Running the Interactive Study Aid Software

The minimum recommended PC configuration for the Interactive Study Aid is as follows:

- A Pentium or better PC
- Microsoft Windows 95

The Interactive Study Aid (ISA) is located on the TPG Companion CD-ROM on the inside back cover of this book. The ISA runs directly from the CD. Therefore, you do not need to install the ISA on your computer's hard drive. The ISA will typically auto-start when you insert the CD into your computer's CD-ROM or DVD-ROM drive. If it does not auto-start, click the Windows Start button, choose Run, and enter x:\isa.exe, substituting your CD-ROM's drive letter (typically d: or e:) for x:.

If the CD-ROM contains only the Interactive Study Aid, the study aid's Startup Screen will appear first. If the CD-ROM contains more than the Interactive Study Aid, the first screen to pop up will allow you to select which program or file you want to access on the CD.

If you have difficulty running the software, you can obtain technical support from LOMA's Help Desk at 770-984-3782 from 8 a.m. to 5 p.m. Eastern Time.

The Help Desk should be contacted only for technical support regarding problems in operating the software. Other comments, including comments about the content of the sample exam, should be sent to:

LOMA
Examinations Department
2300 Windy Ridge Pkwy, Suite 600
Atlanta, GA 30339

or faxed to the Examinations Department at 770-984-3742, or e-mailed to education@loma.org.

Overview of the Interactive Study Aid

In this section, we give you an overview of how the Interactive Study Aid works.

Sample Examination and Practice Questions. The ISA typically includes a Sample Examination as well as chapter-by-chapter Practice Questions. The Sample Exam and Practice Questions are the same as the ones included in the printed manual that accompanies the ISA, but the ISA includes answer choice explanations not found in the printed manual. The answer choice explanations provide you with immediate feedback on why your selected answer choice is correct or incorrect.

Let's run through the steps involved in using the software:

Startup Screen

The first screen that appears when you launch the ISA allows you to tell the software which course you want to study from. The courses are packaged into .ISA files, such as *Study Aid for LOMA 356.isa*. Follow the instructions on the first screen to select your .ISA file, then click the **Next** > button.

Main Menu

The Main Menu appears after the Startup Screen. At the Main Menu, you select whether to study from the Sample Exam or a chapter's Practice Questions. You can also click the **Restart** button on the Main Menu to restart a previously saved study session.

The Main Menu also contains information about the textual materials upon which the course's examination items were based. The first step you should take is to look up the course's current text assignment and ensure that the textbook(s) listed in the software match the current assignment. You should double-check the edition numbers and copyright dates of the textbooks. We want you to be sure that you are studying from the correct textbooks, and with the correct, up-to-date .ISA course file.

You can look up the current course assignment in the LOMA Education and Training Catalog, which is free and available via download from www.loma.org (click on the Downloads button). If you determine that the ISA you are using is based on an out-of-date text assignment, see your Ed Rep to obtain an up-to-date study aid manual for the course. The current CD will be included at the back of that manual.

At the Main Menu, you have the following options:

- **Sample Examination.** This is a full examination similar in content and difficulty level to the actual examination you will sit for.

- **Practice Questions.** These are chapter-by-chapter practice questions that allow you to test your knowledge of each chapter. When you choose the Practice Questions option, you also need to select the textbook and chapter from which to study.

- **View Answer Choice Feedback.** If this option is enabled, then answer choice explanations are available to you. An explanation will pop up each time you select an answer choice. The answer choice explanations appear in the answer choice explanation display.

  Typically, you would want to check this option, so that you get the full benefit of the ISA.

One situation in which you might not want to view the feedback is as a sort of simulation of the actual test-taking experience. Taking the Sample Exam without benefit of the explanations allows you to test your knowledge of the material and preparedness for the real exam.

The ISA also provides you with additional feedback in the form of a green checkmark and a red X. The checkmark indicates a correct answer, and the X indicates an incorrect answer. These graphics appear next to your selected answer choice. This feedback always appears in the Practice Questions, and appears in the Sample Examination if you choose to view the answer choice feedback.

Select the options you want, then click the **Go** > button to continue to the question display.

Question Display

Once you move from the Main Menu into the examination itself, you'll be presented with the question display window. This window displays the current examination question.

Recording your answer. To record your answer to a question, click the round "radio" button immediately to the left of your chosen answer choice, or press the corresponding number key on the computer's keyboard. The question display also contains five toolbar buttons at the top left of the display. Four of these buttons are used for navigating through the examination and are always visible; the fifth is visible when you complete all of the Sample Exam questions or all of a chapter's Practice Questions, and is used to go to the score report.

As long as "Button Help" on the "Options" menu is checked, a help "balloon" will appear below a button when you move the mouse cursor over the button. The balloon gives you a brief explanation of what the button does. Click the Button Help menu option to toggle the button help on and off.

Here is a brief explanation of each of the toolbar buttons:

 Return to the previous question

 Go to the next question

 Choose the number of a question to jump to. You can also jump to a question by clicking the question's number in the question list at the left side of the question display.

 Go to the first remaining unanswered question. Clicking this button causes the software to scan through the exam questions in sequence, to determine the first question for which you have not yet submitted an answer. The program will then take you to that question.

 This button appears only after you complete all of the Sample Exam's questions or all of the current chapter's Practice Questions. Click this button (or choose Get Score Report from the Options menu) to go to the score report.

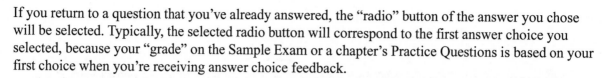

If you return to a question that you've already answered, the "radio" button of the answer you chose will be selected. Typically, the selected radio button will correspond to the first answer choice you selected, because your "grade" on the Sample Exam or a chapter's Practice Questions is based on your first choice when you're receiving answer choice feedback.

This "first-response" grade allows you to judge how well you did on the exam questions without the benefit of the answer choice feedback. Since you'd typically want to keep selecting answer choices until you get the question correct, if the ISA graded your last response, your grade would be 100% every time, instead of being a more accurate reading of how well you knew the material going into the question.

The only exception to the first-response grade is if you choose to take the Sample Examination without viewing the answer choice explanations. Since you do not get the benefit of any answer choice feedback in this situation, the ISA will record your final response.

You can customize the font and font size of the question display panel by selecting **Preferences** from the **Options** menu.

Exam Status. You can get a quick view of how you are doing on the examination by going to the **Options** menu and selecting **Exam Status**. A window will appear that indicates the answers you've selected thus far.

Saving a Session. If you have to interrupt a study session in the software, but want to be able to resume the session later, you can save your progress to a file by choosing **Save** from the **File** menu. In the SaveAs dialog box that appears, choose the drive and/or directory where you want to save the file, enter a name in the "File Name" box, and click the OK button. The software will save the pertinent information it needs to be able to restore your session at a later time.

To resume the session, click the **Restart** button on the Main Menu. In the File Open dialog box that appears, select the drive and directory where you stored the file (it will have a .TST extension), click on the file name, and then click the OK button. The ISA will read in the data from the file and will resume the session where you left off.

Exiting the Exam. To quit the study session at any time, select **Exit to Main Menu** from the **File** menu. Once at the Main Menu, if you want to exit the Interactive Study Aid, click on the Main Menu's **Exit** button.

Completing the Last Question. When you have answered all of the Sample Exam's questions or all of the current chapter's Practice Questions, a message will pop up informing you of that fact. To get your score report after viewing that message, either select **Get Score Report** from the **Options** menu, or click the 'checkmark' button that gets added to the end of the toolbar.

Score Report

This report indicates the number of questions you answered correctly. The score report for a chapter's Practice Questions will show your score on that chapter. The score report for the Sample Exam shows your overall score, and provides you with a chapter-by-chapter grade summary. This chapter-by-chapter summary will show you how well you did on the questions from each chapter. This information will help you to identify those chapters on which you need to focus your additional studies. At an absolute minimum, you should devote some extra study time to those chapters for which your score was less than 70%.

Note that you can view the full chapter-by-chapter grade report ONLY if you complete all of the exam questions.

There are three buttons on the grade report.

Click the **Review the questions I missed** button to return to the study session and rework the questions that you missed. In reviewing the questions you missed, you'll automatically be presented with the answer choice explanations (if such explanations are available), regardless of whether or not you chose the option on the Main Menu to view the explanations. Once you've completed the review, the software will offer you the opportunity to review the questions you missed on the preceding review. You can keep cycling through these reviews of missed questions until you answer all the questions correctly on the first try. You can exit the review at any time by selecting **Exit to Main Menu** from the **File** menu.

Click the **Print my grade report** button to send a copy of your grade report to the printer. A print options dialog box will appear. Select the applicable options for your printer and select OK.

Click the **Exit to the main menu** button to return to the main menu.

For more complete information on using the Interactive Study Aid, see the software's online help file (choose Contents from the Question Display screen's Help menu).

TPG COMPANION CD LICENSE AGREEMENT

This TPG Companion CD License Agreement (the "Agreement") is a legal agreement between You (either as an individual or a single entity) and LOMA (Life Office Management Association, Inc.) for the use of the TPG Companion CD ("the Software") accompanying this Agreement. By using this Software, You are agreeing to be bound by the terms of this Agreement.

Definition of in "Use"

The Software is in "use" on a computer when it is loaded into temporary memory (RAM) or installed into permanent memory (hard disk, CD-ROM, or other storage device) of that computer.

Grant of License

Rights of an Individual. If You are an individual, LOMA grants to You a nonexclusive license to use one copy of the Software on both your office computer and on your home computer provided that You are the only individual using the Software.

Rights of an Entity. If You are an entity, LOMA grants to You a nonexclusive license to use the Software in only one of the following two ways, with the selection to be yours:

- You may designate one individual within your organization to have the sole right to use the Software in the manner provided above under "Rights of an Individual."

- Alternatively, You may install one copy of the Software on a single computer and allow multiple members of your organization to use the Software on that one computer. If You wish to use the Software on another computer, You must deinstall it from the computer it is on before installing it on another computer.

Copyright

The Software is owned by LOMA and is protected by U.S. copyright laws and international treaty provisions. Therefore, You must treat the Software like any other copyrighted material (e.g., a book or musical recording) EXCEPT that You may either make one copy of the Software solely for backup or archival purposes or transfer the Software to a single hard disk provided You keep the original solely for backup or archival purposes. You may not copy the written material accompanying the Software. The questions and instructions and instructional material (hereinafter "the Content") contained in or accompanying the Software are also owned by LOMA and protected by U.S. copyright laws and international treaty provisions. It is illegal to make any copy whatsoever of the Content; to install the Software on a network, intranet, or Web site; to download the Content to another computer or device EXCEPT as expressly allowed under "Grant of License" above; to print screens or otherwise cause the Content to be printed; or to in any other way reproduce the Content contained in or accompanying the Software.

Other Restrictions

You may not rent or lease the Software. You may not reverse engineer, decompile, or disassemble the Software or in any way duplicate the contents of the code and other elements therein.

Disclaimer of Warranty

LOMA MAKES NO WARRANTY EXPRESS OR IMPLIED INCLUDING, WITHOUT LIMITATION, NO WARRANTY OF MERCHANTABILITY OR FITNESS OR SUITABILITY FOR A PARTICULAR PURPOSE. UNDER NO CIRCUMSTANCES SHALL LOMA BE LIABLE TO YOU OR ANY THIRD PARTY FOR ANY INCIDENTAL OR CONSEQUENTIAL DAMAGES WHATSOEVER.

Limitation of Liability

You agree to indemnify and hold harmless LOMA, its employees, its agents, and their successors and assigns against any loss, liability, cost or expense (including reasonable attorneys' fees) asserted against or suffered or incurred by LOMA as a consequence of, or in the defense of, any claim arising from or based upon any alleged negligence, act or failure to act whatsoever of You, your employees, their successors, agents, heirs, and/ or assigns with respect to the aforementioned Software.

LOMA® is a registered trademark of LOMA (Life Office Management Association, Inc.), Atlanta, Georgia, USA. All rights reserved.

ROCKS
MINERALS
AND GEMS

Quarto educates, entertains and enriches the lives of
our readers—enthusiasts and lovers of hands-on living.

www.quartoknows.com

Publisher: Maxime Boucknooghe
Editorial Director: Victoria Garrard
Art Director: Miranda Snow
Designers: Calcium Creative and Jillian Williams
Editors: Calcium Creative and Joanna McInerney

Copyright © QED Publishing 2016
First published in the UK in 2016 by
QED Publishing

Part of The Quarto Group
The Old Brewery
6 Blundell Street
London N7 9BH

A catalogue record for this book is available from
the British Library.

ISBN 978 1 78493 535 1

Printed in China

SAFETY!

Some suggested activities
in this book involve chemicals
which must not touch the eyes,
mouth or skin. When handling
these chemicals, always wear
protective goggles and
gloves and adhere to
safety advice.

PICTURE CREDITS

t=top, b=bottom, l=left, r=right, c=centre, fc=front cover)

Alamy 54c Susan E. Degginger/Alamy Stock Photo
Corbis 9bl Ken Lucas/Visuals Unlimited, 14–15 Allesfoto/
ImageBROKER, 21tc c) Pantafos/Science Photo Library, 30–31
Ben Cooper/SuperStock, 31tr Jonathan Blair, 45t Scientifica,
45b Maurice Nimmo/ **FLPA** 46–47c, 47tr Scientifica, 52b Paul
Andrew Lawrence/Visuals Unlimited, 53tr Visuals Unlimited, 53br
Scientifica, 56 Visuals Unlimited, 63tr Visuals Unlimited, 65b Visuals
Unlimited, 71br Gerald & Buff Corsi/Visuals Unlimited, 72–73c
Lester V. Bergman, 72–73b Scientifica, 74–75cl Visuals Unlimited,
74b Visuals Unlimited, 75c Visuals Unlimited, 75b, 77tr, 91cl
Scientifica, 93t Gary Cook/Visuals Unlimited, 94b Visuals Unlimited,

41br Burnel1, 42–43 Tyler Boyes, 43tr www.sandatlas.org, 43br
Vvoe, 46–47b Dereje, 47br www.sandatlas.org, 48 www.sandatlas.
org, 49t Michal812, 49b Lapas77, 50–51 OlegSam, 51tr www.
sandatlas.org, 51b www.sandatlas.org, 52c www.sandatlas.org,
55c Tyler Boyes, 57tr www.sandatlas.org, 57b Tyler Boyes, 58 Tyler
Boyes, 59t Sementer, 59c Sementer, 59b Tyler Boyes, 60–61 www.
sandatlas.org, 61t Volvio, 61br Tyler Boyes, 62–63 www.sandatlas.
org, 63br www.sandatlas.org, 64b Tyler Boyes, 64–65 kavring,
66–67 LesPalenik, 67tr Arttonick, 67cl Turtix, 67cr Verbaska, 67bl
Imfoto, 68–69 Albert Russ, 69tr MarcelClemens, 69br Miriam
Doerr, 70tr MarcelClemens, 71t Michal812, 71l Albert Russ, 73br
il Fiversnots, 73tr Tyler Boyes, 75t Anastasice71, 76–77 Slobodan

ROCKS,
MINERALS
AND GEMS

JOHN FARNDON

NTENTS

1 ROCKS, MINERALS AND GEMS

Some people think hunting for stones is a bit strange. After all, you find stones all over the place, and most look much the same. But in this book, you'll discover that even the dullest little stone has a wonderful story to tell. And who knows, when you're out hunting for stones, you might just find a precious gem and make your fortune!

A piece of white stone

A chunk of white stone could be limestone. If you look at it through a magnifying glass, you might see shiny white **crystals** of calcite. These tell you that millions of years ago, when the rock began to form, the area where you might be standing was once a **tropical** sea. This is because many sea organisms make their shells from calcite.

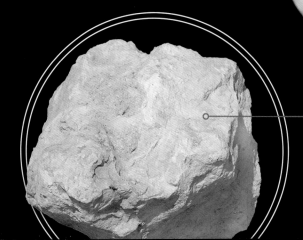

Limestone contains calcite, formed millions of years ago from the shells of sea creatures.

A striped pebble

The stripes on a rock are far more than just an interesting design feature. Those stripes show that the rock is schist. Stripes are signs that the rock was once squeezed so hard and heated so intensely that its very nature changed, and it split into layers.

> The black stripes on this rock tell you that it is schist.

Striking lucky!

Just once in a while, if you're very lucky, you may discover a precious gem while you're out rock-hunting. It doesn't happen very often. **Gems** are indeed rare. But the thrill of discovery is amazing. Even if it is not necessarily a valuable gem, it's exciting to hold such a rare and beautiful thing.

> This is a rough ruby stone. You would be lucky to find rubies, as they are very rare, valuable gems.

A pinky-brown stone

A mottled, pinky-brown stone could be granite. Look closer and you may see different coloured specks of quartz, feldspar and pepper-coloured mica. This stone has come to the surface from where it was made, deep in the fiery heat of the Earth's interior.

> Granite is one of the toughest rocks, surviving longer than most other rocks.

OUR ROCKY EARTH

Our planet is made almost entirely of rock. Earth is one of the four 'rocky' planets of the solar system, along with Mercury, Venus and Mars. It has a small metal core in its heart, but the remaining 85 per cent of it is rock. Earth has a complicated internal structure, as we know by studying the pattern of vibrations from earthquakes. But it is essentially a big ball of rock, so there is no shortage of rocks for you to find.

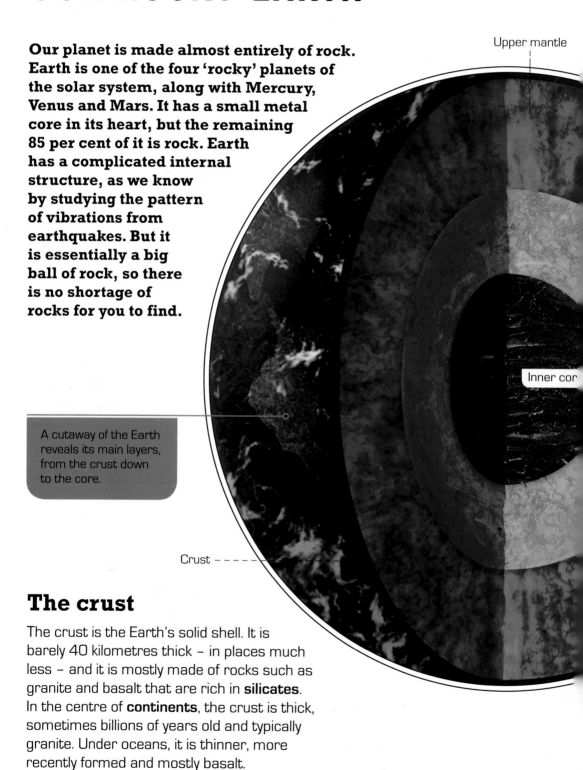

Upper mantle

Inner core

A cutaway of the Earth reveals its main layers, from the crust down to the core.

Crust

The crust

The crust is the Earth's solid shell. It is barely 40 kilometres thick – in places much less – and it is mostly made of rocks such as granite and basalt that are rich in **silicates**. In the centre of **continents**, the crust is thick, sometimes billions of years old and typically granite. Under oceans, it is thinner, more recently formed and mostly basalt.

The upper mantle

Just beneath the Earth's crust is the upper **mantle**, which reaches down to about 670 kilometres below the Earth's surface. It is made mostly of **dense** rock called peridotite. It gets very hot in the Earth's interior, and even in the upper mantle it is warm enough to soften the rock. In places, the upper mantle melts altogether to form **magma**, which then bubbles up through the crust to **erupt** as volcanoes.

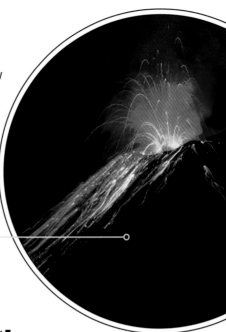

Hot, liquid rock from deep within the Earth erupts on the surface in a volcano.

Lower mantle

ıter core

The lower mantle

From 670 to 2900 kilometres down is the lower mantle. Here, the heat and **pressure** are so intense that silicate **minerals** are changed into dense minerals, such as perovskite and pyroxene. Perovskite is fairly rare on the surface, but since it makes up most of the lower mantle, it actually makes up 80 per cent of the Earth's **volume**.

Perovskite is a mineral that makes up much of the Earth, but is rarely found on the surface.

The outer and inner core

About 2900 kilometres down, the mantle rock gives way to the metal of the Earth's core, which is mostly iron and nickel. The outer core reaches 4200°C, hot enough to keep it permanently **molten**. As the Earth spins, the liquid core swirls around, creating **electric currents** that make the Earth **magnetic**. The inner core is up to 7200°C, but the pressures here are so huge the metal cannot melt.

EARTH'S ROCKY SURFACE

Like a broken eggshell, the Earth's rocky surface is cracked into giant slabs, known as tectonic plates. There are seven giant ones, the size of continents, and dozens of smaller ones. The tectonic plates are not fixed, but are constantly shifting, cracking and drifting. Their movement is so slow that we don't notice it, but it has a dramatic effect on the Earth's surface and the formation of rocks.

Eurasian plate

Imaginary glowing lines show the cracks in the Earth's surface between major tectonic plates.

Philippine pl

Tectonic plates

The biggest tectonic plate is the Pacific plate which lies under almost the entire Pacific Ocean. All the other six big plates – the Eurasian, Indo-Australian, North and South American, African and Antarctic – carry continents, like cargo on a raft. As these plates move around the world, the continents drift with them, continually moving, coming together and drifting apart, so that the map of the world is always changing.

Australian plate

Meeting and parting

Some cracks between plates are divergent, which means the plates are moving apart. This often opens a deep **rift** between them. Some cracks are convergent, which means the plates are crunching together. Often one plate is subducted or shoved under the other. On some cracks, the plates are slowly sliding past each other in opposite directions.

North American plate

Pacific plate

The Great East African Rift Valley is an area where the tectonic plates are gradually moving apart.

Plate boundaries

The boundaries, or cracks, between tectonic plates are where a lot of **geological** activity happens. Here is where most volcanoes erupt and most earthquakes start. Here, too, is where many of the most interesting rocks, minerals and gems are formed. It is not just today's boundaries that are interesting because of the rocks found there. Some rare minerals and gems are brought to the surface in places where boundaries occurred long ago.

The San Andreas Fault runs through California and marks the boundary between the Pacific and North American plates.

THE CHANGING LANDSCAPE

The world's mountains are dramatic proof of the power of geological forces. They have been lifted up thousands of metres by earth movements, then gradually shaped into valleys and brought low again by rain, wind and ice. Mountains weren't created just once, but have been built up and then worn down countless times during the Earth's history.

The Himalayas in South Asia, one of the world's highest mountain ranges, are young and still growing.

Building mountains

Some mountains are lifted up in great slabs by earthquakes. But most of the world's longest, highest ranges were created where the edges of tectonic plates were crumpled up as they crunched together. That's why, like the Andes in South America and the Rockies in the United States, ranges are often long and narrow and full of twisted rock structures.

Mountain formed by crunching plates

Rock layers pushed up

As tectonic plates crunch together, they can throw up layers of rock to form mountains.

Tectonic plate

Tectonic plate

Ancient ranges

All over the world, you can see the remains of great mountain ranges. These ranges were thrown up long ago, but have since been worn down to little more than hills, such as the Appalachians in North America, the hills of Scotland and the Urals of Russia. As these mountains are slowly worn away, the rocks left uncovered prove fascinating sites for the rock-hunter.

DID YOU KNOW?

The Himalayas are being forced higher and higher as the tectonic plate that forms India thrusts into Asia.

The Highlands of Scotland were once high mountains but have been worn down over time.

Growing higher

The Earth's crust floats on its mantle. Mountains are heavy, so the crust sinks deep into the mantle below, like a raft with a heavy load. Every great mountain range has equally deep roots. When rock is worn away from mountain ranges, the mountains become lighter and may bob up, like a raft when you take off some of the load. The Appalachians, for example, worn down long ago, are slowly rising as they become lighter.

The Appalachians in North America are one of the oldest mountain ranges on the planet.

WHAT ARE ROCKS?

Rocks are very hard, solid materials. They come in a variety of different shapes, colours and textures, but they all form in one of three ways: Sedimentary rocks are formed from the loose debris of other rocks, or from organic remains. Metamorphic rocks are changed into new rocks by extreme heat and pressure. Igneous rocks are created directly from molten rocks from the Earth's hot interior.

There are rocks under every landscape, some exposed, some hidden, as you can see in this image of a lake in southern Italy.

Most rocks are made from tiny grains, but they may contain the occasional larger crystal, or phenocryst, such as this black ilvaite.

Crystals in rocks

Look at almost any rock under a magnifying glass or microscope, and you will see that it is made up of countless tiny **grains**. In some rocks, these grains are crystals that fit like a jigsaw because each crystal grew to fill the space around it. These crystals may vary widely in size. Some rocks have unusually large crystals, called phenocrysts, that are **embedded** in a compact **mass** of smaller grains, known as the groundmass.

Rock glue

In some rocks, such as sandstone, the grains do not interlock at all. Instead, they are loosely packed and **cemented** together by a powdery material called a matrix. This sometimes makes the rock crumbly and 'friable'. Stonemasons know that sandstone fresh from the ground is often easy to cut, because the cement is damp and soft. But if the stone is left exposed for too long, the cement dries and hardens, which makes cutting much tougher.

This stonemason is sculpting from damp, fresh sandstone.

Chemical make-up

Rocks are made from the same **chemical elements** as the Earth. Almost half the Earth's crust by weight is oxygen. The oxygen is not in the form of the gas we breathe, though, but bonded into a solid with other elements, such as silicon. Together, oxygen and silicon account for almost three-quarters of the Earth's crust by weight. So rocks are mostly silica, which, in its pure form, is simply sand.

This chart shows the proportion of each chemical element in the Earth's crust.

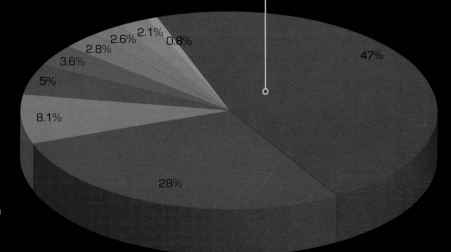

- Oxygen
- Silicon
- Aluminium
- Iron
- Calcium
- Sodium
- Potassium
- Magnesium
- Others

2.1%
2.6%
0.8%
2.8%
3.6%
5%
47%
8.1%
28%

IGNEOUS ROCKS

Nearly 90 per cent of the Earth's crust is made from igneous rocks. There are two kinds of igneous rock: extrusive, or volcanic, and intrusive. Both kinds are created when hot magma wells up from deep in the Earth's interior, then cools and hardens.

How are they formed?

As magma cools, crystals grow in **clusters** in the magma mixture. Different materials in the magma **crystallize** at varying rates, forming many different kinds of igneous rock. The kind of rock that forms depends on the **chemical** make-up of the magma and how the magma **solidified**.

As red hot molten magma cools, it crystallizes and turns to solid rock.

Extrusive igneous rock

Some magmas erupt as **lava** through volcanoes. Rocks that form from lava and other material ejected by volcanoes are called volcanic or extrusive igneous rock. The lava cools so quickly in the open air that the rock hardens before there is time for grains to grow large. So, you can often identify a rock as volcanic if most grains are so fine that you need a magnifying glass to see them. If the rock is dark in colour, too, it's basalt.

Basalt is a dark volcanic rock with very fine grains created by the rapid cooling of magma.

Intrusive igneous rock

Sometimes, magmas cool and solidify underground into large, rocky masses called intrusions. The rock that forms in this way is called intrusive igneous rock. The ground acts as a blanket, so the magma cools slowly and crystals have time to grow quite large. So, if the grains are varied and easy to see, you can tell that the igneous rock is an intrusive rock.

Intrusive igneous rock cools slowly to form grains so large you can see them with your own eyes, as in this diorite sample.

SEDIMENTARY ROCKS

The most common rocks you see on land are sedimentary, because three-quarters of the world's continents are covered by thin layers of sedimentary rock. Most of this is formed from fragments of igneous rocks broken down by the weather. But it can also form from organic remains, such as the shells of sea creatures.

The horizontal lines in the cliffs of the Grand Canyon in the United States are classic signs of sedimentary rock.

How are they formed?

Sedimentary rocks start to form whenever debris, such as sand, mud and organic remains, begins to settle on the beds of seas and lakes, or is piled up by the wind and rivers. As these **sediments** settle, they are buried and **compacted** by the weight of sediments above. Over millions of years, the pressure, combined with the warmth of the Earth's interior, turns the sediments into layers of solid rock.

Identifying sedimentary rocks

It is often easy to identify sedimentary rocks when they are exposed in cliffs, because you can see the layers in which the debris settled (though any earth movement since then may have tilted them at odd angles). This is called stratification. Sometimes you can spot bedding planes – lines that mark breaks in the original settling of debris. Joints are cracks that opened up as the rock dried out and shrank.

Lines in sedimentary rock, called bedding planes, mark where there was once a seabed.

Signs of life

One of the wonderful things about sedimentary rocks is that many contain fossils – the remains of living things **preserved** in stone – along with the rest of the debris. Fossils are like windows into the time and place the rock formed. We know that chalk formed in shallow tropical seas, for instance, because it is studded with fossils of tiny creatures that lived there. Getting to know fossils is one of the best ways to identify sedimentary rocks.

Many sedimentary rocks are rich in the remains of sea creatures caught in the seafloor mud when they died.

METAMORPHIC ROCKS

The searing heat of molten magma or the crushing pressure of earth movements can alter rocks beyond recognition. Just like a cooked cake looks very different from the raw mix, so these cooked and squeezed 'metamorphic' rocks are completely transformed. A soft mudstone, such as shale, is baked and squeezed to create tough grey slate, perfect for roofs. Crumbly grey limestone turns into beautiful, shiny marble.

This glittering marble is a metamorphic rock. It was formed from limestone that metamorphosed under heat and pressure.

Contact metamorphism

Magma in intrusions can reach over 900°C, hot enough to transform any rock it comes into contact with. So, intrusions create an aureole, or ring, of altered, metamorphic rock around them. The closer the rocks are to the intrusion's hot centre, the more they are altered. This alteration by heat alone is known as 'contact metamorphism'.

When subjected to high heat and pressure, this limestone will transform into marble.

Regional metamorphism

The alteration of rocks next to intrusions is **local**, but the huge forces involved in mountain-building can alter rocks over a wide area. This is called 'regional metamorphism.' Near the **fringes**, the change can be mild or 'low grade'. Mudstones may change into similar-looking slate. But in the heart of the mountain belt, the extremes can turn that same mudstone into shiny gneiss.

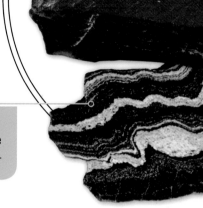

Increasing pressure and heat turn mudstone (top) first to slate (middle), then to gneiss (bottom).

Canada's shield

Beneath Canada lies a vast mass of tough, incredibly ancient rock known as the Canadian Shield. It is over 2.5 billion years old. It also contains some of the largest and oldest formations of metamorphic rock in the world, with vast **terranes** of ancient granulite and quartzite. It is rich in valuable minerals such as nickel, gold, silver and copper.

The Canadian Shield is made from vast areas of tough and very old metamorphic rock.

ROCK CYCLE

...ins and hills look so solid, it seems they
...there forever. Yet all the world's landscapes
...ng reshaped as they are attacked by the
...r and worn down by seas, rivers or glaciers.
...mes, the shift is sudden and dramatic, as in a
...de. Mostly, it is too gradual to see. But in time,
...ace rocks are broken down to make way for
...ks, in a process called the 'rock cycle.'

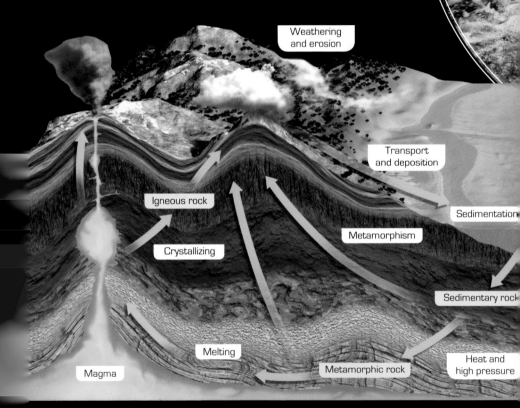

Weathering and erosion

Transport and deposition

Sedimentation

Igneous rock

Metamorphism

Crystallizing

Sedimentary rock

Melting

Heat and high pressure

Magma

Metamorphic rock

recycling

...k material can come up from deep in the Earth as magmas.
...t surface rocks, especially sedimentary rocks, are made from
...ts that are continually recycled. A grain may be **weathered**
... rock, become part of another, then be weathered out again
...es over, for long periods. Grains in rocks near the **margins** of
...ts can be recycled often; grains in rocks deep in the interior

Rocks through time

There are many paths a grain can follow through the rock cycle. Wind and rain may break up igneous rock into grains that are washed by rivers to settle on the seabed. They are then compacted with other grains to form a sedimentary rock. This rock may then be exposed to heat and pressure, turning it into a metamorphic rock, which may, too, be broken down in time.

These boulders were once part of a slab of rock that fell in the river and has been worn down by the water.

Rocks are broken down by waves, weather and water, and the debris forms new rocks.

Round and round

Most studies suggest the grains in rocks in the **continental crust** came up from the Earth's interior over 2.5 billion years ago. Yet they make up rocks that are generally much, much younger. They have just been recycled many times.

2 ROCK-HUNTING

The great thing about hunting for rocks is that it hardly costs anything. All you need to start building up a collection is a pair of sharp eyes so you can see loose specimens when you are out walking, and a good book to help you identify what you find. Of course, if you become keen on rock-hunting, there are a few items of equipment that will come in handy (see page 40).

Just looking

Most people interested in rocks think they should build up a collection. But why not simply look, as bird-watchers do, without actually picking up a chunk of rock and taking it home? It may be quite enough to record your finds in a notebook and take a photo or make a drawing, leaving the specimen in its natural place.

Some rock-hunters prefer to leave specimens in their natural place.

DID YOU KNOW?

Collecting and identifying stones is an ancient human activity. Stone Age people learned that certain stones could be shaped to make tools, and that the best stones were found in certain locations.

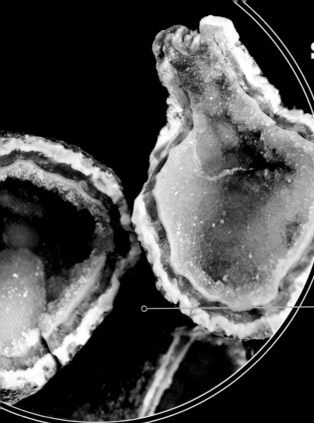

Swapping

It is really exciting to find your own rock samples, but if you can only find a limited range in your own neighbourhood or the places where you go on holiday, you could think of swapping specimens. What may be normal for you might be a real rarity for other collectors! Look online for one of the many rock swap clubs.

Swapping rocks with other collectors means you may come across some unusual specimens to add to your collection, such as these geodes.

Buying rocks

Some rock enthusiasts don't even bother to go out hunting for samples in the field. They prefer to buy from collectors' shops. Some just browse the Internet and purchase online to build up their collection without ever moving from their chair. There is no reason why you can't do both: collect samples for yourself, then add to your collection with samples found by others.

Always get adult supervision before you purchase anything online.

WHERE TO HUNT FOR ROCKS

You can see rocks and minerals almost everywhere. Houses may have roofs of slate. Kitchen work surfaces may be made of granite. Statues may be made of marble. But if you want to build your own collection, you'll need to hunt for samples in the countryside at rock outcrops and deposits.

Rock outcrops

The best outcrops are cliffs by the seashore or in mountain areas. Here, you can find fallen rocks sitting loose at the cliff base. You may even be able to chip samples out of the cliff face. But take care of rock falls, and always wear a helmet. (See page 40 for more about keeping safe.)

DID YOU KNOW?

One of the most amazing rock outcrops is Uluru in Australia, a giant oval lump of rock, 354 metres high, that pokes above the surface of a huge underground sandstone bed.

Mountains and rocky beaches, such as here in the Isle of Skye, Scotland are good places to find rock samples.

Rock deposits

Deposits are places where lose stones lie. Beaches are probably the best deposits. The sea has done all the work breaking solid rock into sample stones. Powerful waves can move sand considerable distances. But bigger stones are almost certainly local, which should help you to identify them.

Placer Deposits

Nature often helps the rock-hunter by sorting minerals. Stones that survive the break-up of the rock they came from tend to be made of tougher minerals. Grains of heavy minerals may gather in **shoals** in streams because they are the first to sink when the **current** slows down. These are called 'placer deposits.' Since gold, copper and precious gems such as emeralds are naturally dense, placer deposits are great sites to hunt for samples.

People often find gold in placer deposits by sifting them with a pan.

ROCK LANDSCAPES

Every type of rock tends to create a particular kind of landscape. Some rocks create landscapes that are so distinctive you can identify the rock from far away. The relationship between rocks and landscapes is complicated. But, with a little experience, you can begin to identify what rocks and minerals are likely to occur in a particular area, simply from the lie of the land, or the details on a map.

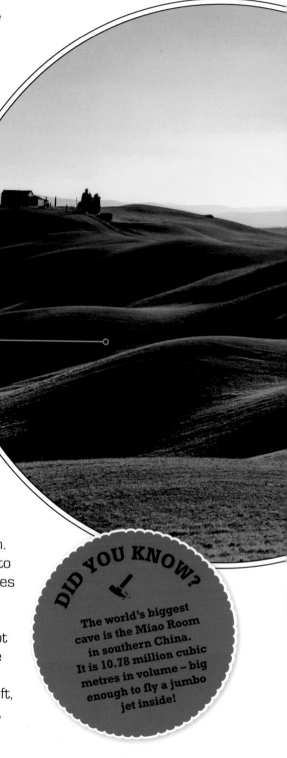

Water moulds the surface of rocks such as clay into smoothly rounded hillocks, as seen here in Tuscany, Italy.

Chunky v. smooth

Most sandstones are permeable. This means they let water soak through them. Since little water flows over the surface to wear them smooth, sandstone landscapes tend to be chunky, often with bare rock outcrops. Clays and shales are impermeable, meaning that water cannot soak through them. Water is kept on the surface, which wears them into gently rolling landscapes. Clays are also very soft, so tend to get worn away to form valleys, while hard sandstones form hills.

DID YOU KNOW?

The world's biggest cave is the Miao Room in southern China. It is 10.78 million cubic metres in volume – big enough to fly a jumbo jet inside!

Karst landscapes

Limestone often forms a landscape that looks as if it has been blasted by a bomb. It is known as **karst**, after the Karst Plateau in Slovenia. Rain water is slightly **acidic**, and as it trickles down through the joints between limestone blocks, it **dissolves** the rock away. Over millions of years, the joints are carved out into wide **cavities** and caves, which may eventually collapse to form **gorges**.

This illustration shows a slice into limestone, and the cavities opened up where acidic rain water has dissolved away the rock.

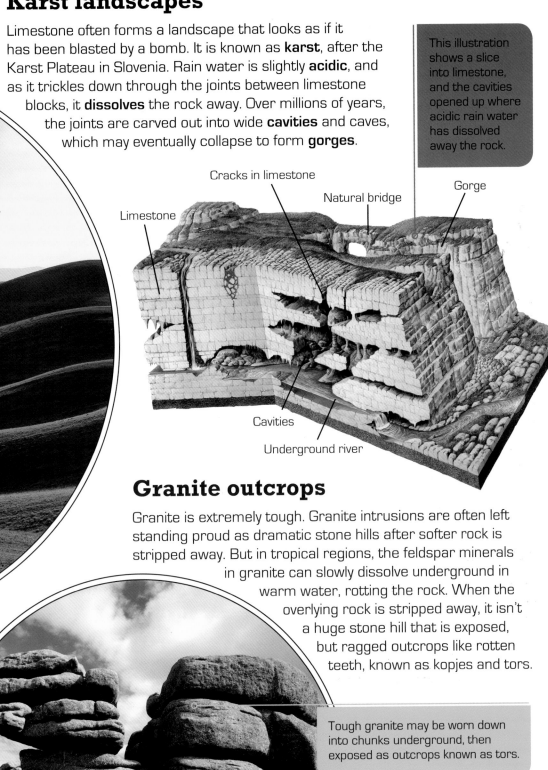

Cracks in limestone

Natural bridge

Gorge

Limestone

Cavities

Underground river

Granite outcrops

Granite is extremely tough. Granite intrusions are often left standing proud as dramatic stone hills after softer rock is stripped away. But in tropical regions, the feldspar minerals in granite can slowly dissolve underground in warm water, rotting the rock. When the overlying rock is stripped away, it isn't a huge stone hill that is exposed, but ragged outcrops like rotten teeth, known as kopjes and tors.

Tough granite may be worn down into chunks underground, then exposed as outcrops known as tors.

READING THE LANDSCAPE

Every stone tells a story. Some of that story is revealed by identifying the stone and reading about its history. Yet even when you don't know exactly what stone it is, you can use your detective skills to follow up some clues. Sometimes, the story is connected to how an individual stone came to be where it is. At other times, the story is about how an entire rock outcrop came to be.

Old v. new

If you find a sharp shard of stone, the chances are it is likely to be **scree**, shattered from the cliff above by frost within the past year or so. Rounded pebbles on a beach or a stream bed are much older. They are round because, for thousands of years, they have been rolled around and worn smooth by rough sand in the water. That is why pebbles on a beach are generally round.

Shards of rock are likely to be scree, fallen quite recently from cliffs above.

A round pebble has been worn smooth over time by river or sea water.

Looking for clues

You can often see the **sequence** of layers in which sedimentary rocks were laid down – one on top of the other, with the oldest at the bottom. Using clues like fossils, you can read their history, identifying things such as the changing environment in which the rocks formed.

By identifying which fossils occur in different rock layers, you can build up a sequence of local rock formation.

Breaks in the sequence

Geologists often look for tell-tale breaks in rock sequences. If you see an ingenous intrusion cutting clean across a sequence of sedimentary rocks for instance, you know it is quite young – because it must have formed after even the youngest rock in the sedimentary sequence. Another break in the rock sequence is an 'unconformity', where rocks of one sequence lie directly on top of a different one. In an 'angular' unconformity, the sequences meet at an angle: This is because slanting older layers were sliced flat before newer layers formed.

A dramatic change in the direction of rock layers, seen here just above the centre, is an unconformity.

THE AGES OF ROCKS

Sedimentary rocks are laid down one on top of the other. If they were never disturbed, you could slice a column right through them to reveal the entire history of the Earth like a book. Although you can't find anything like this anywhere, it is a useful way of thinking about the history of rocks, back to Cambrian times 545 million years ago, when the first widespread fossils date from.

Geological time

Just as a day is divided into hours, minutes and seconds, so geologists divide the Earth's history into time periods. The longest are eons, thousands of millions of years long. The shortest are chrons, a few thousand years long. In between come eras, periods, epochs and ages. For geologists, the most important are periods, lasting 30–60 million years.

Precambrian
The first life forms (bacteria) appear and give the air oxygen

Quaternary
Many mammals die out in Ice Ages; humans evolve
1.8 million years ago

Tertiary
First large mammals; birds flourish; widespread grasslands
65 million years ago

Cretaceous
First flowering plants; the dinosaurs die out
142 million years ago

Jurassic
Dinosaurs widespread; archaeopteryx, earliest-known bird
205.7 million years ago

Triassic
First mammals; seed-bearing plants spread; Europe is in the tropics
248.2 million years ago

Permian
Conifers replace ferns as big trees; deserts are widespread
290 million years ago

Carboniferous
Vast warm swamps of fern forests which form coal; first reptiles
354 million years ago

Devonian
First insects and amphibians; ferns and mosses as big as trees
417 million years ago

Silurian
First land plants; fish with jaws and freshwater fish
443 million years ago

Ordovician
Early fishlike vertebrates appear; the Sahara Desert is glaciated
495 million years ago

Cambrian
No life on land, but shellfish flourish in the oceans
545 million years ago

CENOZOIC

MESOZOIC

PALEOZOIC

USING FOSSILS

There are fossils in nearly every sedimentary rock, preserved there for millions of years. Different plants and animals lived at different times and in varying conditions. By identifying certain fossils within the rock, you can learn a lot about when and how the rock was formed.

A fossilized Alethoptreis fern shows the rock is from the Carboniferous period.

How do fossils form?

When a sea creature such as a shellfish dies, its body rots away, but its shell falls to the seafloor and is buried in mud. Over millions of years, the shell **dissolves** away. The dissolved chemicals **recrystallize** within the cavity left behind, leaving a perfect **replica**, the fossil, of the shellfish's shell.

Rock dating

Some **species** lived only at a certain time. So by identifying where in the rock sequence they appear and where they disappear, you can tell if one rock layer is older than another. For instance, rocks containing fossils of a species that died out 220 million years ago are clearly older than rocks containing species that only appeared 150 million years ago.

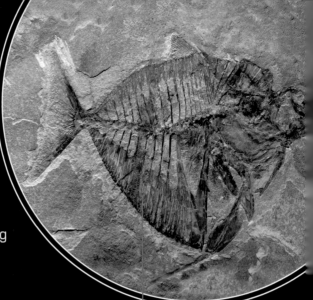

Rock matching

Geologists often try to track rock formations across wide areas by looking for repeated appearances of the same **assemblage** of fossils. You may see two rock outcrops thousands of kilometres apart. But if they contain exactly the same range of fossils, you know they formed at the same time.

When fossils are as clear as this fish, it is usually easy to work out how old the rock is, using a guide to fossil ages.

Index fossils

Dinosaur fossils may be exciting, but they are not much use for rock-hunters because they are so rare. What rock-hunters need are easy-to-spot fossils that are found all over the place. These key fossils, known as index fossils, must be small and show marked changes through time. This is why all index fossils are small sea creatures, such as ammonites and trilobites.

Ammonites are common fossils that show clear changes over millions of years. They therefore make good index fossils.

GEOLOGICAL MAPS

Learning to use a geological map is one of the rock-hunter's most useful skills. A geological map shows what rocks occur where, along with the main geological features. This not only helps you quickly identify rock and mineral samples on the ground, it also means you can work out just where you are likely to find good samples of particular minerals.

This geological map section shows the variety of rocks and features found in an area of Klamath Falls, Oregon, United States.

Solid geology

Most geological maps you are likely to come across show 'solid' geology – the pattern of solid rocks just below the surface. This gives you a great idea of what rocks you are likely to see exposed in cliffs and **quarries**. Maps like these are also helpful to geologists in finding the rock structures most likely to produce mineral **ores** and oil and gas deposits.

Colour code

Geological maps are colour coded to help identify the different kinds of rock in the ground:

- Igneous rocks
- Sedimentary rocks
- Limestone
- Metamorphic rocks

3D modelling

Geologists often use special computers to help them identify geological features. These computers can construct 3D virtual models of the rock formations in the ground, which can be turned to be viewed at any angle.

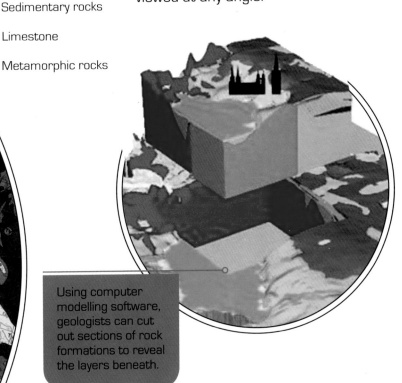

Using computer modelling software, geologists can cut out sections of rock formations to reveal the layers beneath.

These crimson areas show us there is igneous rock just below the surface.

A cross-section shows the rock layers below the ground.

Cross-section

One of the best ways to understand the way rocks are occurring is with a cross-section. This is a slice down through the ground showing how the rock layers lie. Most maps have one or two key cross-sections. A black line drawn across the map indicates where the cross-section has been taken.

10,000 feet = 3048 meters

VERTICAL EXAGGERATION X2

COLLECTING ROCKS

You may find that hunting for rocks and minerals is exciting enough, and that you're quite happy to put the specimens you pick up into a box and get ready for the next trip. But once you've got more than a few samples, you may find you want to store and arrange your collection more carefully.

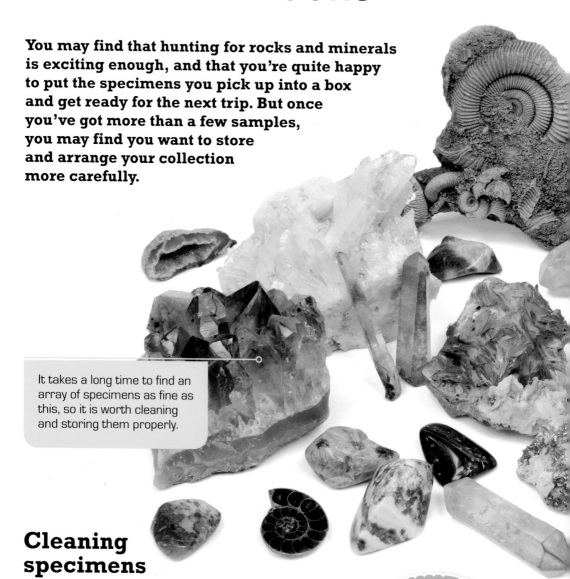

It takes a long time to find an array of specimens as fine as this, so it is worth cleaning and storing them properly.

Cleaning specimens

Most specimens are filthy when they come out of the ground, and should be cleaned before storing them. Take care you identify them first, since some minerals, such as halite, are soluble – they will dissolve in water. Test the sample first with a dab of water before wetting it. If it is soluble, clean it with a soft toothbrush or dab it with pure alcohol. Unwanted calcite and lime can be dissolved away with mild vinegar.

DID YOU KNOW?

Some minerals, such as copper and silver, oxidize quickly (change colour in the air). Others, like borax, dry out. These minerals should be stored in airtight containers.

Brush and rinse

To clean **insoluble** samples, brush off any loose dirt with a soft toothbrush. Then rinse the sample in warm (not hot) water, with a drop of **detergent** to shift greasy stains. Most specimens are quite delicate so only use a hard nailbrush on tough minerals like quartz, and never chip off dirt with a screwdriver. Stubborn dirt can usually be removed after soaking in water overnight.

Simple household items like these are all you need to clean your rock specimens.

Containers that stack on top of each other are useful for storing samples safely and neatly.

Storing your collection

Store your specimens in a cool, dry, dark place, spaced apart, perhaps in little cardboard or plastic boxes. You can arrange them in the groups indicated in this book, but always label each carefully with the following details:

1. The mineral or rock name

2. The chemical or mineral composition

3. The group it belongs to

4. Where you found it precisely

5. The kind of rock formation where you found it

6. The date you found it

ROCK-HUNTING TOOLKIT

You can start a rock and mineral collection simply by picking up stones when walking in the countryside or by the sea. But if you want to get serious, a backpack equipped with a few basic tools is a great help.

Hammer and chisel

The rock-hunter's key tools are a hammer and chisel. You can manage with an ordinary builder's hammer and chisel, but proper geological ones are much better. The golden rule, though, is to keep hammering to a minimum. The hammer should mostly be used for splitting stones, not for breaking stones out of cliff-faces.

Gloves, a helmet and a geological rock hammer, are essential for rock-hunters.

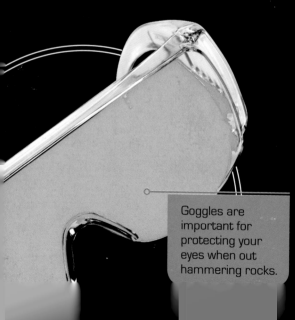

Goggles are important for protecting your eyes when out hammering rocks.

Keeping safe

Rocks are hard and sharp, and rock outcrops can be dangerous places, so it is vital to pay attention to safety. Rocks can splinter when hit, so always wear goggles when hammering. Tough gloves are also useful for handling sharp-edged samples. A helmet could save your life from falling rocks when out hunting near cliffs.

Making a record

Smartphones make life much easier for the rock-hunter. You can use phones to photograph rocks and samples on site and they will automatically use GPS to record the location. Use a notebook, though, to make a clear note of where you found samples, and use sticky labels to identify them.

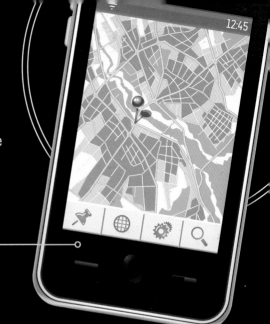

Use a smartphone to take photos and record locations.

Carrying samples

You'll need a strong bag for your samples. A small backpack is ideal, since it leaves your hands free to pick up rocks. Fill it with bubble-wrap or paper to stop your samples from knocking together.

A strong bag is useful for collecting samples and a good magnifying glass can help you better identify them.

Closer look

The best way to really get to know your rocks and minerals is to study them closely through a magnifying glass. That way you can see the individual grains and crystals. Use a glass that gives five to ten times magnification. A more powerful magnifying glass gives a restricted view, while a weaker one is little help.

3 ROCK DETECTIVE

All rocks look much the same at first glance, but once you know what to look for, you'll find it quite easy to identify most rock samples, or at least their family group. The idea is to narrow it down step by step. Begin by identifying if it is sedimentary, igneous or metamorphic.

DID YOU KNOW?

You can often identify a sample from the rocks around it. Samples found near a cliff with layered rock are probably sedimentary. Mottled, grey-pink rocks found near a tor could be granite.

Sedimentary

Sedimentary rocks are a pale, dull, even colour, made from similar, compacted grains held together by cement. They may crumble when you rub them. Look, too, for bedding planes and fossils. Decide on whether the rock is **clastic** or **biochemical**. Clastic rocks are generally dark brown or yellowish. Biochemical rocks are paler – white, cream or grey.

Rock Identifier

Breccia is a large-grained, clastic sedimentary rock. Clastic rocks have different grain sizes.

Grains too small to see:
siltstone, claystone, shale, marl, chert

Small grains:
sandstone, ironstone, greensand, arkose, greywacke

Large grains:
breccia, conglomerate, boulder clay

Examples of biochemical rocks:
chalk, limestone, dolomite

Metamorphic

Metamorphic rocks can appear like igneous rocks, but look for banding, which is never found in igneous rocks. Metamorphic rocks tend to be smooth, even and shiny. Igneous rocks are more mottled and rough-looking.

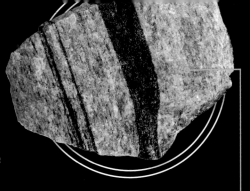

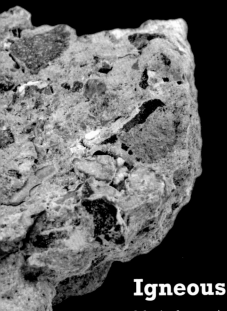

Rock Identifier

Gneiss is a banded metamorphic rock with visible grains.

Examples of banded metamorphic rocks:

Grains small to see:	**Visible grains:**
slate, phyllite, mylonite, blueschist	schist, biotite mica schist, granulite, gneiss

Examples of non-banded metamorphic rocks:

Too soft to scratch glass:	**Hard enough to scratch glass:**
marble, dolomite, greenstone, serpentinite	hornfels, metaquartzite, eclogite, amphibole

Igneous

Made from closely interlocking crystals, igneous rocks have a hard, shiny, mottled look. They almost never have layers or bands. To identify an igneous rock, look at how dark it is and how coarse the grains are. The paler it is, the richer in silica and the more acidic it is likely to be. The deeper below ground it formed, the slower it cooled and the coarser the grains.

Rock Identifier

Andesite porphyry is a medium-grained, igneous rock.

Examples of igneous rocks:
Fine-grained: pale – rhyolite, medium – andesite/trachyte, dark – basalt

Medium-grained: pale – quartz porphyry, medium – andesite porphyry/monzonite, dark – dolerite

Coarse-grained: pale – granite, medium – diorite/syenite, dark – gabbro

SANDY VOLCANIC ROCKS

Most volcanic igneous rocks are formed when lava erupts from volcanoes. They are always fine-grained because the lava cools too quickly for big crystals to form, although you see spots of larger crystals within them. In rocks that form from violently erupting volcanoes on the ocean margins, lots of silica is mixed in as the magma oozes up, making the rocks sandy in colour.

Rhyolite

Rhyolite is a common volcanic rock made from the same silica-rich magma as granite. But this magma only forms rhyolite after erupting through explosive volcanoes, such as Mount Tambora in Indonesia. Rhyolite is usually light pink or reddish-brown. It can look like granite because it contains large phenocrysts that formed underground before it erupted. You may need to look through a microscope to see the fine grains.

Rock Identifier

Type: Rhyolite
Grain size: Fine
Composition (what it's made of): Quartz, feldspar, mica
Formation (how it was formed): Lava flows, dykes (wall-like formations of igneous rock), volcanic plugs (hardened lava)
Colour: Pale pinkish brown

Mount Tambora, seen here from above, is an active volcano in Indonesia. When it erupts, its silica-rich magma forms rhyolite.

DID YOU KNOW?

In 1815, Mount Tambora erupted and caused the most powerful volcanic explosion in history. It was heard 2000 kilometres away, on the island of Sumatra.

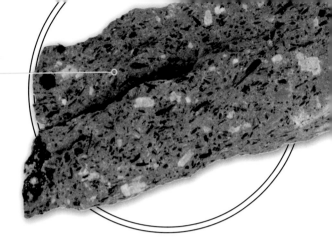

Dacite

Dacite is the tough rock you often see in road chippings, but it can be beautiful when polished. The magma it is made from is not quite as thick and silica-rich as rhyolite. It is a very pale, sandy-coloured rock with a reddish or greenish tinge. It often wells up inside old volcanoes, forming **lava domes** like Mount St. Helens in Washington, United States.

Andesite

Andesites are the most common volcanic rocks after basalt. They get their name from the Andes mountains in South America. Many explosive, cone-shaped volcanoes, such as Japan's Mount Fuji, are powered by andesite magmas. Andesite lava erupts to create thick lava flows and domes of andesite rock. Andesite's silica content falls halfway between rhyolite and basalt. You can often identify it from its classic 'salt and pepper' look, with white feldspar grains (the salt) set in a dark groundmass of glassy minerals, such as mica.

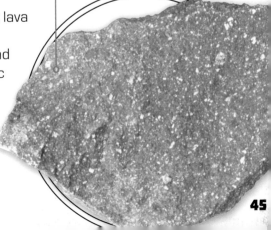

DARK VOLCANIC ROCKS

When magma oozes up through continents, it becomes richer in silica, making it thick and sticky. But where magma flows up through the thinner crust under the ocean, it contains far less silica, and flows freely. The magma floods out from the ocean floor as lava in huge quantities, forming vast sheets of dark volcanic rock.

Rock Identifier

Type: Basalt
Grain size: Fine
Composition: Feldspar, pyroxene, olivine, magnetite
Formation: Lava flows, dykes, sills
Colour: Black

Basalt

Basalt is the most common rock in the Earth's crust by far. It makes up 70 per cent of the entire ocean floor. Not all basalt is found under oceans. It can flood out of volcanic **fissures** on land too, forming India's Deccan Traps and North America's Columbia River plateau. It is even darker than andesite, and fine grained. Like dacite, it is used widely in road chippings covered in **tar**.

Basalt can be found on the four rocky planets; Mercury, Venus, Earth and Mars. Even the dark splodges on the Moon are basalt.

Obsidian

Jet black and shiny, obsidian is one of the most beautiful of all rocks. It forms when rhyolitic lava erupts and cools so quickly that there is no time for crystals to form. It can be polished and sharpened into a knife blade.

Pumice and tuffs

Not all volcanic rocks are formed from lava. Pumices form from the froth of lava. Tuffs, which look similar to pumice, form from ash and fragments of solid magma. Pumice is so full of holes that it is incredibly light, and is the only rock that floats. To see if a rock is pumice, throw it in water. If it floats, it is pumice. Geologically, the rock is light enough to float only for a short while. In time, the holes fill with minerals and it becomes heavy.

IGNEOUS ROCKS UNDERGROUND

Some magmas approach the surface but never erupt. Instead, these intrusions cool and solidify into rocks underground. The rocks that form here are known as hypabyssal. Their grain size is midway between fine-grained volcanic rocks, which cool rapidly above ground, and coarse-grained plutonic rocks, which cool slowly underground.

Rock Identifier

Type: Monzonite
Grain size: Medium
Composition:
Feldspar, pyroxene,
hornblende,
quartz, mica
Formation: Sills and
other small intrusions
Colour: Dark grey,
mottled

Monzonite

Monzonite forms at medium depth underground. It has medium grain size, medium silica content and is only slightly acidic. It looks very much like granite at first glance, but contains far fewer white chunks of quartz.

DID YOU KNOW?

South Africa's Bushveld Complex is the world's largest sill-like intrusion. It contains huge resources of platinum, palladium and vanadium ore, along with a lot of chromium, iron and tin.

Syenite

The Roman historian Pliny gave the name syenite to the rocks quarried by the Ancient Egyptians at Syene on the Nile. Although the rocks at Syene are granites, the name syenite was used by 19th-century German geologists to describe similar-looking rocks. Syenites form in similar places to granite and are sometimes described as plutonic rocks. But they contain far less quartz than granite, and often form dykes and other shallow intrusions.

Rock Identifier

Type: Syenite
Grain size: Coarse to medium
Composition: Feldspar, mica, hornblende, pyroxene
Formation: Dykes and other small intrusions
Colour: Light pink, grey, white mottled

Quartz porphyry

Porphyries are igneous rocks that contain very large crystals. Quartz porphyries are rocks that form from the same magma as rhyolite and granite, but contain large spots of white quartz. They are usually hypabyssal and form in dykes. However, they can also form far deeper underground and also in lavas on the surface. Famous examples are in the Swiss Alps and England's Charnwood Forest.

Porphyry was the purple-red rock used for building Roman palaces and statues.

Rock Identifier

Type: Quartz porphyry
Grain size: Mixed
Composition: Quartz, feldspar, mica
Formation: Dykes and ancient lava flows
Colour: Light brown with large white spots

IGNEOUS ROCKS FROM DEEP DOWN

Plutonic igneous rocks are formed from hot masses of magma deep underground called plutons. The biggest plutons are huge domes called batholiths. Insulated from the air by thick layers of rock above, these masses take a long while to cool. Crystals have plenty of time to grow, and so plutonic rocks are tough rocks with chunky grains.

Granite

Granite is one of the toughest of all rocks. Long after other rocks have crumbled away, batholiths of granite are left standing like islands in the sea. Granite is generally light-coloured, speckled rock. It is made from a mix of white or pink feldspar, white quartz and dark brown mica or muscovite, in grains big enough to be seen with the naked eye.

Rock Identifier

Type: Granite
Grain size: Coarse and granular
Composition: Quartz, feldspar, mica, hornblende
Formation: Batholiths
Colour: Pale, mottled pink, brown or grey with dark specks

Diorite

Diorite is similar to andesite, but it forms deeper underground and has coarser grains. It usually forms when granite is **contaminated** by **impurities**. It usually forges in batholiths with granite along continental margins. It is a grainy rock made mainly of plagioclase feldspar and hornblende, without the creamy grains of quartz in granite.

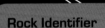

Rock Identifier

Type: Diorite
Grain size: Even-grained, porphyritic
Composition: Feldspar, mica, hornblende
Formation: Dykes and small plutons
Colour: Speckled black and light

Gabbro

Named after the village of Gabbro in Tuscany, Italy, gabbro is the coarse-grained equivalent of basalt and dolerite. It is common in the ocean crus and often forms in giant sheet-like intrusions called lopoliths. It looks like diorite but is darker.

Rock Identifier

Type: Gabbro
Grain size: Very coarse-grained
Composition: Feldspar, pyroxene, olivine
Formation: Sills and lopoliths (saucer-shaped intrusions)
Colour: Black with white

DYKES, SILLS AND VEINS

From every igneous intrusion, fingers of magma ooze out through the rock around. Some push their way into cracks to form dykes. Some magma slides between rock layers to form sills. As the intrusion cools and shrinks, fluids collect in cracks that open up, forming veins.

Dolerite

Dolerite (also known as diabase) is one of the most common dyke and sill rocks, forming the famous Palisade sill in New Jersey, United States. You can identify dolerite by its dark greenish colour and its medium grain size.

Rock Identifier

Type: Dolerite
Grain size: Medium
Composition: Feldspar, pyroxene, olivine, mica, magnetite
Formation: Dykes and sills
Colour: Dark, greenish grey or black

Pegmatite

Pegmatites are formations rather than a kind of rock. Veins and **lenses** of solidified fluid cool slowly around igneous intrusions to form spectacularly large crystals, at least the size of a grapefruit. The smallest pegmatites are the size of a bed; a few are the size of a large school. Pegmatites are the source of many wonderful gems, from topaz to tourmaline.

Aplite

Aplites are the palest of all igneous rocks, and look just like raw sugar. They form in veins and dykes and are basically granite without the dark mica, made from just quartz and feldspar. There are aplite veins in almost every granite intrusion. They form at the last stages and at the lowest temperature of any igneous rock, so they cool very quickly. This is why they are unusually fine-grained for an intrusive rock.

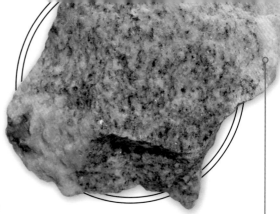

Rock Identifier

Type: Aplite
Grain size: Fine
Composition: Quartz, feldspar
Formation: Veins and dykes in granite intrusions
Colour: White or pale pink

Lamprophyre

The name lamprophyre comes from the Greek for 'glistening mix' and it looks just like a lump of brown sugar that has been dipped in coffee. It is the only rock that forms solely in dykes, typically near intrusions of tonalite and granodiorite.

Rock Identifier

Type: Lamprophyre
Grain size: Mixed
Composition: Variable
Formation: Dykes
Colour: Dark grey or brown with black spots

Rock Identifier

Type: Pegmatite
Grain size: Super coarse
Composition: Quartz, feldspar and 550 other minerals
Formation: Lenses, dykes, veins
Colour: Pale pink, whiteish

DID YOU KNOW?

The island of Elba in Italy is home to some amazing pegmatites. Although mostly now stripped of their best crystals, they were once the source of beautiful tourmalines.

ROCKS FROM DEBRIS: CLAYS AND MUDS

Wherever there are rolling hills and gentle valleys, the rocks beneath them are often sedimentary rocks made from debris. The fragments that make up this debris are called clasts. Swept along by rivers and wind, clasts settle everywhere from the seabed to deserts, where, over millions of years, they pile up and are compacted into clastic rock.

Claystone and mudstone

Clastic rocks made from powder-fine fragments such as clay, mud and **silt** are known as lutites. In claystone, the grains are so tiny you can only see them with a magnifying glass. This makes the rock feel smooth and slippery when wet, and is what makes clays so useful. They can be shaped into anything from building bricks to tea cups. Most claystones form in shallow sea water, and are dotted with fossils of tiny sea creatures.

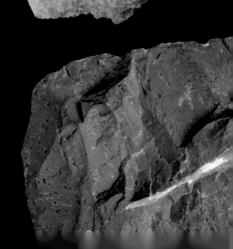

Rock Identifier

Type: Claystone (above) and mudstone (right)
Grain size: Ultra-fine
Composition: Quartz, feldspar and mica powder
Formation: Clays and muds settling offshore and on river floodplains
Colour: Black, grey, green, white, red

Shale

Shale is formed by layers of mud and clay that has settled on the beds of seas and lakes. The shale is then squeezed into thin layers called laminations. It looks flaky like slate but is softer, and is studded with fossils. Oil shales are black shales rich in the minerals kerogen and bitumen. When heated, they produce oil in a process known as fracking.

Rock Identifier

Type: Shale
Grain size: Ultra-fine
Composition: Quartz, feldspar and mica powder
Formation: Clays and muds settling offshore and on river floodplains
Colour: Black, grey, white, brown

Siltstone

In siltstone, some of the grains are large enough to see, and the rock feels gritty. The grains are heavier than clay, which means they are not carried as far out to sea, so siltstones form closer to the shore. The rocks often show the ripple marks of currents. Beneath the Great Plains of North America are huge deposits of siltstone.

DID YOU KNOW?

The Oxford and London clays of England were the source of many of the great fossil finds in Victorian times. The finds, such as this plesiosaur, led to the discovery that dinosaurs existed.

Rock Identifier

Type: Siltstone
Grain size: Fine
Composition: Quartz, feldspar and mica powder
Formation: Clays and muds settling offshore and on river floodplains
Colour: Pale grey, beige, with bands

ROCKS FROM DEBRIS: SANDSTONES AND BRECCIAS

Like claystones and mudstones, sandstones and breccias are clastic sedimentary rocks, made from debris. The grains, which are large enough to be easily seen by the naked eye, are made mainly of quartz and feldspar. They are so tough they can go on forming rocks for millions of years.

Rock Identifier

Type: Sandstone
Grain size: Sand-sized
Composition: Quartz, feldspar fragments
Formation: Everywhere sediments settle, from deserts to seabeds
Colour: Variable, typically sandy grey, yellow, brown or red

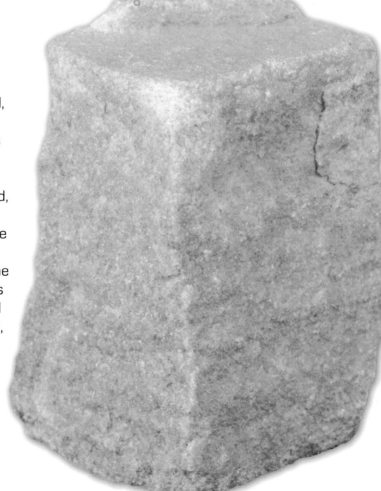

Sandstone

Sandstone is made from cemented grains of sand, piled up by desert winds, or on beaches, riverbeds and seabeds. The shape of the grains gives a clue to where the rock formed, with the roundest grains forming in the desert. The colour comes from the material that cements the grains. Some sandstones are stained brown or red with the iron-rich mineral, haematite.

Orthoquartzite

Orthoquartzites are almost entirely made of different sized grains of quartz, from the sand piling up where waves crash on a beach.

Rock Identifier

Type: Orthoquartzite
Grain size: Sand-sized
Composition: Quartz
Formation: Sand on beaches
Colour: White, pale grey

Wackes

Wackes are also made from sand. But while sandstone is made entirely from sand-sized grains, wackes are a **chaotic** mix of sand, clay, silt and even small stones. Greywacke (pictured here), from the German word for 'grey grit', was formed from the debris of **avalanches** under the sea.

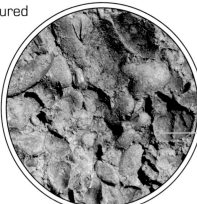

Rock Identifier

Type: Wackes
Grain size: Very mixed
Composition: Quartz, feldspar and mica, clay and stones
Formation: Undersea avalanches
Colour: Grey, green brown

Conglomerate

Rock Identifier

Type: Rudite: breccia and conglomerate
Grain size: More than 2mm (gravel and stones)
Composition: Hugely variable, but quartz is common
Formation: Fast rivers, avalanches
Colour: Variable

Breccia

Rudites: Breccias and conglomerates

Rudites are clastic rocks made from large fragments. Breccias are basically piles of debris turned to stone. They form near the source of the debris in sudden events, such as avalanches. Conglomerates form slowly from loose, rounded pebbles piled up by rivers.

ROCKS FROM LIVING REMAINS

Not all sedimentary rocks are made from rock fragments. Some are made from minerals dissolved in water that settle to form chemical sediments. Others are made entirely from the remains of living things. All sedimentary rocks contain some fossils, but organic rocks, such as limestone and chalk, are made from almost nothing else.

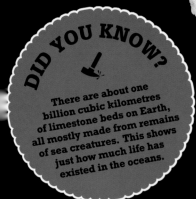

DID YOU KNOW?

There are about one billion cubic kilometres of limestone beds on Earth, all mostly made from remains of sea creatures. This shows just how much life has existed in the oceans.

Chalk

Milky white and so soft you can write with it, chalk is made from almost pure calcite. Around 100 million years ago in the Cretaceous period, billions of tiny **algae** left their remains known as coccoliths, along with the shells of creatures called foraminifera, on the seabed. Over millions of years, they built up into thick beds of chalk

Rock Identifier

Type: Chalk
Grain size: Fine-grained
Composition: Calcite
Formation: From the remains of marine algae and tiny shells
Colour: White

Limestone

Limestones are made from white **calcium carbonate** (calcite or aragonite) grains. In some limestones, the calcite comes more from the fossils of sea shells, **corals** and **plankton** that lived long ago. Some, such as reef and shelly limestone, are made almost entirely of fossils. In other limestones, the calcite settled chemically.

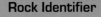

Rock Identifier

Type: Limestone
Formation: From sea shells and bone and precipitation of dissolved calcite
Grain size: Clay or sand-sized
Composition: Calcite and aragonite
Colour: White, grey, cream

Oolitic limestone

Oolitic limestones are made from tiny balls of mostly calcium carbonate known as ooliths. They are sometimes known as roestone, because they look just like fish roes, or eggs. Ooliths are tiny grains of silt rolled to and fro in lime-rich mud made from the remains of sea creatures.

Rock Identifier

Type: Oolitic limestone
Grain size: Smaller than sand
Composition: Calcium carbonate
Formation: Tropical seabed
Colour: White, grey, cream

Dolostone

Dolostone looks just like limestone but is chemically different. Limestone is made mainly from calcium carbonate; dolostone is at least half made from magnesium carbonate (the mineral dolomite).

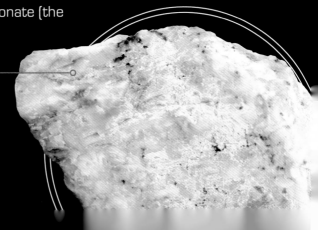

Rock Identifier

Type: Dolostone
Grain size: Sand-sized
Composition: Quartz
Formation: Effect of magnesium-rich sea water on limestone
Colour: White, pale grey

ORGANIC ROCKS AND EVAPORITES

Unlike the sedimentary rocks that are made from grains, chemical rocks, called evaporites, are formed entirely from dissolved minerals. Mineral-rich waters evaporate, leaving behind solid deposits. Organic rocks, such as coal, are not made from grains either, but from the compressed remains of plants.

Tufa

Tufas are calcite deposits that build up around mineral-rich springs, rather like limescale builds up around the taps in areas of hard water. Unlike travertine, it has a slightly spongy texture. In places, the same lime-rich waters drip from the ceilings of caves, creating icicle-like **stalactites**, or drip on the floor, creating pillar-like **stalagmites**. Together they are called dripstones.

Rock Identifier

Type: Tufa
Grain size: Powdery
Composition: Calcite
Formation: From lime-rich waters, typically at cool springs
Colour: White, buff

Travertine

Travertine, found at hot springs, is tougher than tufa. It often comes as a pale honey-coloured rock that sculptors sometimes use instead of marble. The Ancient Romans used travertine for making statues. The 17th-century Italian sculptor Bernini used it to build the famous colonnade of St. Peter's Square in Rome. In the United States, Yellowstone National Park is well known for its travertine terraces.

Rock Identifier

Type: Travertine
Grain size: Powdery
Composition: Calcite
Formation: From lime-rich waters, at hot springs
Colour: Pale honey

DID YOU KNOW?

Over seven billion tonnes of coal is mined from the Earth and burned each year. More than three billion tonnes comes from China alone.

Coal

The only rock that burns, coal is made from the remains of plants that grew mainly in the Carboniferous and Permian periods. Over time, these remains were squeezed and changed into solid **carbon**. The deeper they were buried, the more compacted they were and the richer in carbon they became. The deepest, blackest coals are anthracites, which are so high in carbon that they burn almost without smoke. Brown coals and peat are low in carbon and burn smokily.

Rock Identifier

Type: Coal
Grain size: Fine
Composition: Carbon and organic chemicals
Formation: Squeezed remains of swamp plants
Colour: Black, brown

CONTACT METAMORPHIC ROCKS

Magma oozing up through the ground is so hot that it can cook any rock it comes into contact with. The heat melts and reforms crystals in the rock, changing it into metamorphic rock. Around every magma intrusion, there is a circle of altered rocks. The closer to the intrusion the rocks are, the more they are altered.

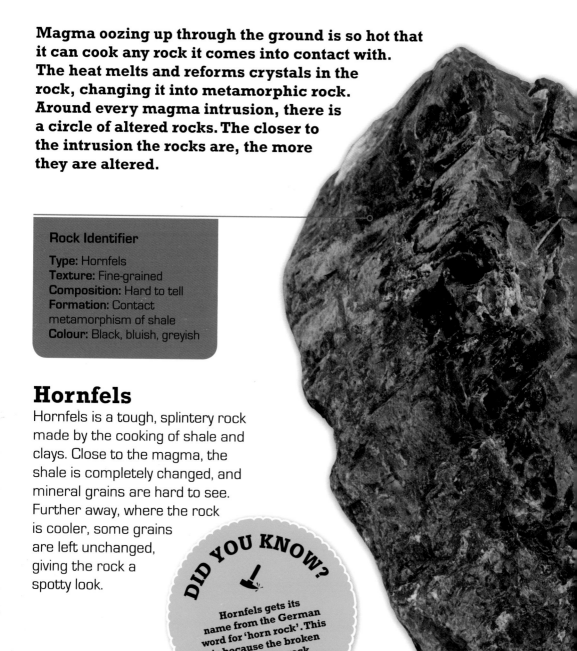

Rock Identifier

Type: Hornfels
Texture: Fine-grained
Composition: Hard to tell
Formation: Contact metamorphism of shale
Colour: Black, bluish, greyish

Hornfels

Hornfels is a tough, splintery rock made by the cooking of shale and clays. Close to the magma, the shale is completely changed, and mineral grains are hard to see. Further away, where the rock is cooler, some grains are left unchanged, giving the rock a spotty look.

DID YOU KNOW?

Hornfels gets its name from the German word for 'horn rock'. This is because the broken edges of the rock can look like animal horn.

Marble

When limestone is cooked by contact with
magma, it turns into marble. Marble is a beautiful
rock, especially when polished. The colour ripples
come from impurities. Marble can also form under pressure
deep within the roots of mountains. The most perfect white
marble is Carrara marble from Italy. Pure limestone is as
white as icing sugar.

Quartzite

Quartzite looks like the brown sugar version of marble,
but it is made from sandstone, not limestone, so it
is mostly quartz, not calcite. Its colour depends
upon traces of iron oxide. Quartzite is one of the
toughest rocks. Unlike marble, you cannot scratch
it with a coin. Quartzite outcrops standing bare
can often be seen long after weaker
rocks around them have been
worn away.

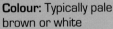

REGIONAL METAMORPHIC ROCKS

Regional metamorphic rocks are transformed over large areas by the crushing pressures of mountain building. The degree of pressure, from low grade (mild) to high grade (severe), creates different rocks from the same original rock. Under extreme pressure, the rock develops layers or stripes, known as foliation.

Slate

Slate is a smooth, dark grey rock that splits easily into layers, making it quite brittle. It has been used for hundreds of years to make roof tiles, because it is surprisingly **weather resistant** and can be broken into flat sheets. Slate is created by low-grade regional metamorphism of shale and mudstone.

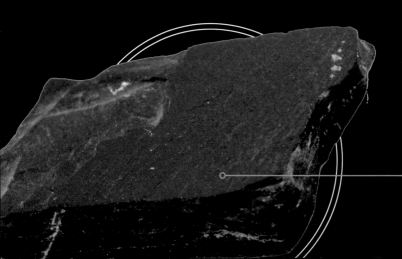

Rock Identifier

Type: Slate
Texture: Very fine-grained
Composition: Mica and chlorite
Formation: Low-grade regional metamorphism of shale
Colour: Grey, black

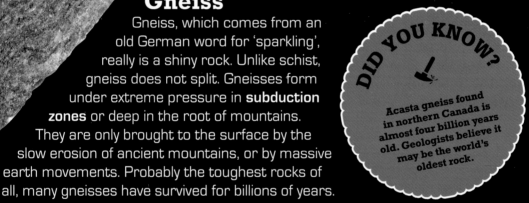

Schist

Schist has striking grey or black stripes. It forms when shale and mudstone come under quite severe pressure. This pressure turns shale first into slate, then a rock called phyllite and finally, schist. In schist, mica crystals are forced to grow in line with the pressure, creating **schistosity**.

Rock Identifier

Type: Schist
Texture: Fine, medium grain
Composition: Mica and chlorite
Formation: Medium-grade regional metamorphism of shale
Colour: Greenish grey, black stripes

Gneiss

Gneiss, which comes from an old German word for 'sparkling', really is a shiny rock. Unlike schist, gneiss does not split. Gneisses form under extreme pressure in **subduction zones** or deep in the root of mountains. They are only brought to the surface by the slow erosion of ancient mountains, or by massive earth movements. Probably the toughest rocks of all, many gneisses have survived for billions of years.

DID YOU KNOW?

Acasta gneiss found in northern Canada is almost four billion years old. Geologists believe it may be the world's oldest rock.

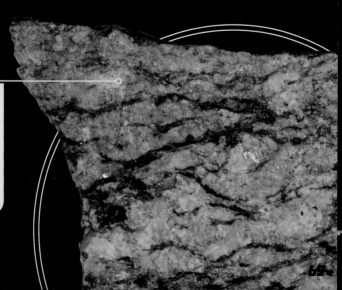

Rock Identifier

Type: Gneiss
Texture: Medium to coarse grained
Composition: Mica and chlorite
Formation: High-grade regional metamorphism of almost any rock
Colour: Grey, pinkish, with dark stripes

4 MINERAL-HUNTING

Since rocks are made of minerals, you might think the best places to find minerals are the same places you hunt for rocks. That is partly true, but most of the minerals in rocks are tiny grains that are not very interesting to a mineral collector. But you can learn to identify special places where large and interesting crystals grow.

Veins, like these pink quartz veins, are good places to find minerals.

Veins

Vein minerals form from hot fluids from magma that are injected into cracks in rocks.

Examples of vein minerals

Bornite	Galena	Marcasite	Topaz
Calcite	Gold	Sphalerite	Tourmaline
Cassiterite	Magnesite	Sulphur	
Feldspar	Magnetite	Rhodochrosite	

Pegmatites

Pegmatites are small, rare rock formations that form from the last, mineral-rich stages before magma solidifies.

Examples of pegmatite minerals

Apatite	Beryllium	Lithium	Tin
Beryl	Garnet	Rubidium	Tourmalines

Cavities in pegmatites include:

Aquamarine Fluorapatite Heliodor Topaz Spessartine

Pegmatites are the host rock for many minerals, including these garnet crystals.

Spinel is one of the rare gems that forms directly from a volcanic melt.

Igneous intrusions

Primary minerals form directly from a volcanic **melt**, rather than from other minerals. They include:

Examples of primary minerals

Apatite	Ilmenite	Rutile,
Augite	Muscovite	Sodalite
Biotite	Nepheline	Spinel
Enstatite	Olivine	Topaz
Hornblende	Quartz	

Pockets in sediments

Diagenetic minerals are new minerals that form pockets in sedimentary rocks.

Examples of diagenetic minerals

Barite	Chalcedony	Pyrite
Calcite	Chrysocolla	Pyrolusite
Celestine	Smithsonite	Turquoise
Cerussite	Sphalerite	Witherite

Salt lakes and hot springs

Evaporite minerals form when minerals are **precipitated out** of cool **solutions**.

Examples of evaporite minerals

Anhydrite	Gypsum	Sylvite
Borax	Halite	Ulexite

Turquoise can be a diagenetic mineral, forming at the same time as sedimentary rocks.

The whole of the Earth's crust is made of minerals. However, large, collectable crystals are rare, which is why they are so exciting to find. Minerals form in one of four ways:

1) from slowly cooling magma

2) from chemicals dissolved in fluids

3) as other minerals are altered chemically

4) as other minerals are squeezed and heated in rocks that undergo metamorphism.

Minerals from magma

Molten magmas are a mix of chemicals. As they cool, certain chemicals begin to join and crystallize. The crystals grow as more **atoms** attach to them. The minerals with the highest melting points crystallize first. But it is what is left behind, known as 'late-stage' magmas, that form the most interesting crystals. As these magmas solidify, they leave mineral-rich fluids that may crystallize to form gems. For example, fluids rich in fluorine form topaz.

Minerals from water

Water can only hold a limited amount of chemicals dissolved in it. When it reaches its saturation point, or limit, chemicals start to solidify. This can happen when water cools or evaporates. When water rich with minerals dissolved from rocks collects in **lagoons** and lakes, it evaporates, leaving some minerals behind. Other minerals form from **hydrothermal solutions**

These large green fluorite crystals grew slowly in a fluid that was still semi-liquid.

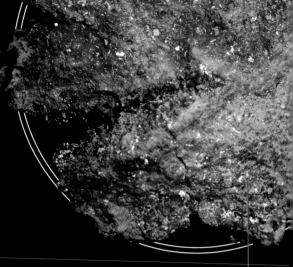

Minerals altered chemically

As soon as minerals form, their chemical make-up starts to change. Some, such as diamonds, can take billions of years. Others change very quickly. Many metal minerals are altered by moist air, such as iron minerals, which **rust**. Some mineral crystals, such as cuprite, form where water seeps down through rocks.

Cuprite crystals form where water seeping through rocks comes into contact with copper minerals.

Minerals in metamorphic rocks

When rocks are subject to metamorphism, the minerals in them are altered. They melt, then recrystallize as different minerals. Rocks known as 'skarns' that contain lots of rare minerals form like this, as do rubies.

Uncut, even crystals of rubies look less than perfect.

MINERAL CRYSTALS

Mineral crystals form bit by bit as atoms attach themselves, just as icicles grow as the water on them freezes. Crystals have chunky, geometric shapes. Although crystals are rarely perfectly shaped, they do develop in a small range of patterns. Knowing these patterns can help you identify a mineral.

Galena belongs to the cubic crystal system.

Crystal systems

All crystals have some degree of symmetry – they look the same shape from different angles. There are six basic symmetrical shapes or 'systems'. The simplest is a cube. Crystals of each mineral tend to adopt one of these systems.

Orthorhombic: like a stubby matchbox or prism shape.

Cubic: simple cubes and octahedrons (8-sided shapes) and dodecahedrons (12-sided shapes).

Triclinic: like a twisted matchbox with the edges cut off; hard to see the symmetry.

Tetragonal: like a long box, but the corners may be shaved off.

Monoclinic: like a tablet.

Hexagonal and trigonal: Hexagonal crystals have six sides; trigonal have three.

Crystal habit

Individual crystals grow in a cluster. The typical form this cluster takes for each mineral is known as its 'habit.' The habit can help you identify a mineral. Sometimes, minerals grow in solid masses in which there are no individual crystals. This is called a 'massive habit'. The habit often depends on the growing conditions.

Examples of habits:

Acicular: needle-like clusters	**Drusy:** a mat-like coating	**Globular:** ball shapes
Bladed: clusters of thin flat crystals	**Fibrous:** thin, fibre-like crystals	**Reniform:** shaped like kidneys
Dendritic: like tree branches	**Foliated:** in thin leaves	**Rutilated:** needles inside a crystal

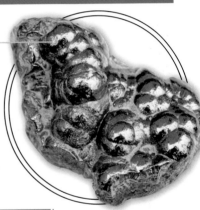

Haematite has a reniform crystal habit, shaped like kidneys.

Scolecite crystals have a needle-like, acicular habit.

This gold specimen shows a dendritic habit, like tree branches.

HARDNESS, CRACKING AND DENSITY

You can identify each mineral from its characteristics. Minerals can be hard or soft, brittle or flexible, dense or light. Hardness is the simplest clue to a mineral's identity. You can test hardness using a system called Mohs' scale. You can work out density, or heaviness, using a spring balance.

Hardness and Mohs' scale

To test a mineral's hardness on Mohs' scale, you will need 10 standard minerals, one for each grade of hardness (see the pictures below), or use the substitutes suggested.

First, take a sample and try to scratch a mark on another sample. Repeat this with each sample to find out which will scratch, and which can be scratched. Then, place each mineral on Mohs' scale. For example, if your sample can be scratched by apatite (5) but not by fluorite (4), its hardness is 4.5 on Mohs' scale.

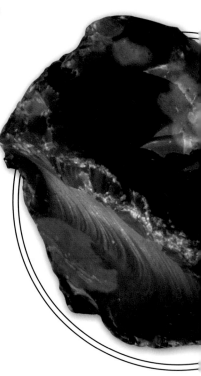

These minerals are ordered according to Mohs' scale, starting with the softest (talc), and ending with the hardest (diamond).

1. Talc

2. Gypsum (or a fingernail)

3. Calcite (or a bronze coin)

4. Fluorite (or an iron nail)

5. Apatite (or glass)

Cleavage

You can sometimes identify a mineral by its 'cleavage' – the number of ways it cracks or breaks:

| One way: it breaks into flat sheets |
| Two-way: it breaks into planks |
| Three-way: it breaks into blocks |
| Four-way: it breaks at angles into chunks |

These terms are also often described in more detail, such as 'perfect in four ways' or 'good in one way'.

Mica 'cleaves' just one way, into flat sheets.

Density

Geologists measure density in 'specific gravity' (SG). This is a mineral's density relative to water. For example, the SG of gypsum is about 2.3. Corundum, a denser mineral, has an SG of 4.

To measure specific gravity, you need a spring balance.

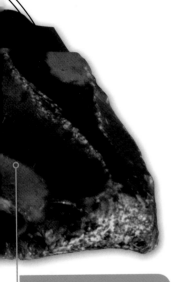

The distinctive way flint breaks in curves is known as conchoidal fracture, named after conch sea shells.

Here is how you measure SG:

1) Hang your sample on a spring balance and take a measurement of its weight.

2) Plunge the sample, still on the spring balance, in a large bowl of water. Take another measurement.

3) The SG is your first measurement, divided by the difference between the two measurements.

6. Feldspar (or a penknife blade)

7. Quartz (or a stainless steel knife)

8. Beryl (or sandpaper)

9. Corundum (or a corundum knife sharpening tablet)

10. Diamond

MINERAL COLOURS

Colour is often the first thing you notice about minerals. Some have such striking colours, like red ruby, that it is easy to think you can identify a mineral from its colour alone. But colour can be misleading. Most minerals actually have little colour in their pure form. They get their colours from traces of other chemicals, so the same mineral can be different colours.

Colours

Some minerals have their own pure, natural colour. These minerals, including blue azurite and pink rhodochrosite, are known as idiochromatic. Most minerals, however, are allochromatic. This means they get their colour from tiny impurities.

When minerals such as fluorite and sodalite are placed under UV light (see the main picture), they glow in different colours to normal (shown in the smaller picture, right.) This glow is called fluorescence.

Streak test

No matter what impurities it contains, you can sometimes find the true colour of a mineral by doing a 'streak' test. Just rub the mineral hard across the unglazed back of a porcelain tile to see what colour streak it makes.

To make a streak test, rub your sample across the unglazed underside of a white bathroom tile. This hematite is showing a reddish brown streak.

Lustre

Lustre is the way a mineral looks and reflects light. The terms geologists use to describe lustre include: vitreous (shiny like glass); dull; waxy; greasy; silky; metallic; resinous (like glue); and adamantine (sparkling).

Serpentine has a waxy lustre.

Transparency

Some mineral crystals are as clear as glass. Others, such as chrysoprase, are translucent – they let light glow through, but you can't see through them. Opaque minerals like galena and serpentine block out light altogether.

Quartz is usually translucent, but occasionally it can be almost as clear as glass.

DID YOU KNOW?

Crystals can give amazing tricks of the light. Iridescence is a shimmering effect, asterism is a star effect, and opalescence is a rainbow-coloured sheen.

GEMS

Large, colourful and sparkling gems are rare and highly prized. They include diamonds, rubies, emeralds and sapphires. Of the 4,000 or so minerals, only 130 form gems, and only around 50 of them are commonly used. Jewellers look for four qualities in a gem: clarity, cut, colour and carat.

DID YOU KNOW?

The Cullinan Diamond was a huge gem found in the Premier Mine in South Africa by Thomas Cullinan in 1905. It weighed 3106 carats, or 0.6 kg, and was almost as big as a baked potato!

Once cut and polished, gems look very different to how they did in the ground.

Where do gems form?

Gems only form in very unusual conditions, which is why they are so rare. They can form in volcanic pipes, or be found in them, like diamonds in veins of rock called kimberlite. They can form in the late stages of a magma intrusion, as in pegmatites, which produce gems such as tourmalines, sapphires and rubies.

Clarity and cut

Clarity is the most highly prized quality in a gem. A good gem is perfectly **transparent** and sparkles brilliantly as light is reflected inside it. The best diamonds have a special internal brilliance known as 'fire'. This can only be seen when the diamond is specially cut and polished.

Diamonds have to be specially cut and polished to reveal their true sparkle and 'fire'.

Colour

A rich colour is what makes some gems so special, like blue sapphires and green emeralds. But many gems come in a variety of colours. Some colour varieties are much more valuable than others and even have their own special name. Sapphire is simply the blue version of the mineral corundum (see page 94), while ruby is the red version.

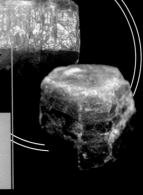

Straight from the ground, sapphires can look like blue sugar lumps.

Carat

The size of a gem is given in carats. In the ancient world, gems were weighed with seeds of the carob tree, which are amazingly constant in weight. Later the carob seed became the basis of a weight unit called a carat, which is about a fifth of a gram. Any diamond weighing more than one carat is valuable.

IDENTIFYING MINERALS: WHAT DOES IT LOOK LIKE?

There are many thousands of minerals. Just a handful, like malachite and crocoite, are unmistakable. Most of the rest are much harder to tell apart. You often need to go through all the clues step by step before you can make a firm identification.

A bright green could be malachite (below). Clear greens could be emerald, olivine or dioptase.

Colour ID

Some minerals have striking colours that may help you identify them straightaway. Here are some examples:

Blues include azurite (left), chalcanthite, lazulite and chrysocolla.

Reds include scarlet crocoite (above), pinky red rhodochrosite, dark red cuprite, vermillion cinnabar and blood red jasper.

Yellows include golden pyrite and marcasite, custard orpiment (below), and yellow sulphur.

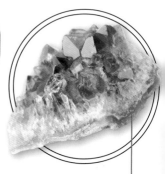

A purple could be amethyst (above).

Make two groups

You can divide minerals into two groups: those with metallic lustre and those without. The number of minerals that have a non-metallic lustre is bigger.

Minerals like quartz never have a metallic lustre.

Simple tests

With most minerals the colour varies too much to make a good identification. Luckily, its streak is always the same. So, start with a streak test and follow this by testing the mineral's hardness on Mohs' scale. This should narrow the possibilities down to six or fewer minerals with the same streak and hardness. You can then measure their specific gravity to make a final identification.

To make it easier to begin identifying a mineral with streak, you could go through this book and make a note of all the minerals with each colour of streak: white, yellow to brown, orange, green, blue, red, black.

Chalcopyrite is a mineral with metallic lustre.

IDENTIFYING MINERALS: WHERE DID YOU FIND IT?

You can tell a lot about a mineral from where you find it. For example, particular minerals are often found together with the same other minerals. This means that you may be able to identify a mineral by the minerals you find with it. Similarly, each mineral tends to form in particular situations, such as veins or pegmatites.

Blue azurite and green malachite is one of the most striking of all mineral partnerships.

Associations

Minerals that are found together are said to be associated. The chart (right) shows some common associations. Some associations are minerals formed from a particular kind of rock, such as the quartzs, feldspars and micas in granite. Others are linked to particular kinds of mineral-forming environments, such as veins.

Some common mineral associations:
Purple amethysts with golden or clear calcite
Blue azurite with green malachite
Honey-coloured barite on yellow calcite
Blue celestine with yellow sulphur
Purple fluorite with black sphalerite
Golden pyrite with milky quartz
Green apatite in orange calcite
Silver galena with yellow anglesite and sparkling cerussite

Signposts

Once you get to know associations, you can learn how to use more common minerals as signposts to lead you to other minerals. For example, if you spot a vein of calcite and barite, don't pass it by. Calcite and barite veins usually contain the lead and zinc ores galena and sphalerite.

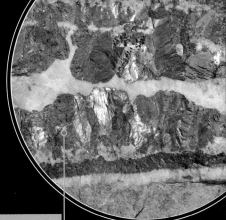

Following a calcite or barite vein could lead you to sphalerite and galena.

Assemblages

Some associations happen because particular mixes of minerals form at the same time, such as when rocks form in particular conditions, or when magma cools and sets. When shale is **metamorphosed** to form hornfels, for example, the minerals in it change to garnet, sillimanite, feldspar and biotite mica. Mixes like these are called **assemblages**.

Water changes

Some associations can be found where water seeped into the ground. Minerals are dissolved in the water near the surface, then they are re-deposited lower down. When water seeps through pyrite ores, for example, it creates first sulphates, then carbonates, then malachite and azurite, and finally chalcocite, covellite, chalcopyrite and bornite.

When schist changes in certain conditions, it can create pockets of mica and aventurine feldspar.

5 MINERAL DETECTIVE

Quartz is a silicate mineral, and the second most common mineral on Earth, after feldspar.

Minerals are not easy to identify just by looking at them. The difference between them is mostly in their chemistry. This is why minerals are usually arranged into different chemical groups. A few are native elements that are found naturally as pure, single elements. All the rest are compounds that combine two or more elements.

Native elements

About 20 minerals are **native** elements. These include metals such as gold, silver and copper, **semi-metals** such as arsenic and non-metals such as sulphur and diamond.

Gold is one of the most distinctive and precious of all native elements.

Sulphides and sulphosalts

These are made from a combination of sulphur and a metal, or a metal-like **substance**. They include some very important metal ores, such as galena (lead ore) and cinnabar (mercury ore).

Oxides and hydroxides

Combined with oxygen and a metal, or a metal-like substance, these vary from hard gems such as ruby and sapphire, formed deep underground, to softer earths such as bauxite that form nearer the surface.

Halides

Halides are formed from a combination of metals and a halogen element – chlorine, bromine, fluorine and iodine.

Sulphates, chromates and molybdates

These are made from a combination of a metal with oxygen and either sulphur, chrome or molybdenum. Sulphates such as gypsum are all soft, pale and translucent or even clear.

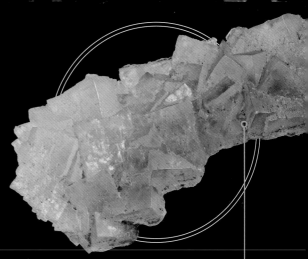

Halides, like halite, are soft and dissolve easily in water.

Phosphates, arsenates and vanadates

These form from a combination of a metal with oxygen and either phosphorus, arsenic or vanadium, and by alteration of other minerals.

Carbonates, nitrates and borates

These are made from a metal with oxygen, combined with either carbon, nitrogen or boron. Carbonates, such as calcite, form mainly by the alteration of other minerals, from hydrothermal solutions and on the seabed.

Silicates

There are more silicates than all other minerals put together. They are made from a combination of a metal with oxygen and silicon. Over 90 per cent of the Earth's crust is made from silicates such as quartz and feldspar.

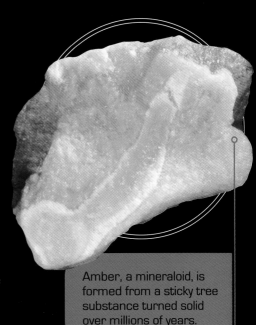

Mineraloids

Some naturally occurring solids are made by living plants or creatures, or from their remains. These organic materials include amber, opal, jet and coal.

Amber, a mineraloid, is formed from a sticky tree substance turned solid over millions of years.

NATIVE METALS

Native elements occur mostly as metals, such as copper and silver. Some, such as diamond and gold, are very long lasting. They may survive long after the rock they came from has been broken up. If you are very lucky, you might find native metals washed up in streams.

MINERAL IDENTIFIER

Type: Copper
Crystal system: Isometric
Habit: Wiry branching masses
Colour: Copper, with green tarnish
Streak: Copper
Lustre: Metallic
Hardness: 2.5-3
Cleavage: None
SG (Specific Gravity): 8.9+

Copper

The sunset red colour of copper is unmistakable. When it is tarnished (exposed to air), copper is a distinctive bright green. Often you can find copper from a green stain on rocks known as 'copper bloom'. If you scrape off the stain, you will see the glowing copper beneath, but pure copper is rare.

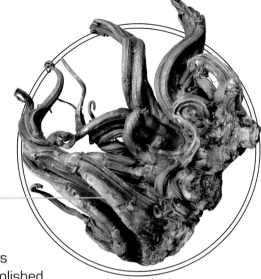

MINERAL IDENTIFIER

Type: Silver
Crystal system: Isometric
Habit: Wiry branching masses
Colour: Silver, with black tarnish
Streak: Silver-white
Lustre: Metallic
Hardness: 2.5-3
Cleavage: None
SG (Specific Gravity): 10-12

Silver

Like gold, silver is beautiful when polished. But when exposed to the air, it quickly **tarnishes**. This is why it is not easy to spot in the ground. Silver grows in wiry, dendritic masses, like twisted branches. Silver, like gold, is usually found in hydrothermal veins, associated with galena (lead ore), zinc and copper. But unlike gold, it is rarely found in rivers.

MINERAL IDENTIFIER

Type: Gold
Crystal system: Isometric
Habit: Grains or nuggets
Colour: Golden yellow
Streak: Golden yellow
Lustre: Metallic
Hardness: 2.5-3
Cleavage: None
SG (Specific Gravity): 19.3 +

DID YOU KNOW?

Five per cent of all the gold ever found in the world is now stored below the streets of New York, in the United States' central bank known as the Federal Reserve.

Gold

Gold is very rare but very special. It does not often form compounds, and almost never **corrodes**. Pure gold is found naturally in rocks, and stays shiny, yellow and **untarnished** almost forever. This is why it was one of the first metals ever used. It is usually found in **hydrothermal veins** in igneous rocks, where it is associated with quartz and sulphide minerals such as stibnite. You may also find it as grains or nuggets in rivers.

DIAMOND AND SULPHUR

Most native elements are metals, but there are two which are not: carbon and sulphur. Carbon can be found in various forms, including diamond, graphite and carbynes. Carbon is a hugely important mineral. Carbon compounds are the chemicals from which every living thing is made. They are also the basic chemicals in fuels such as oil, coal and gas.

Sulphur

Native sulphur is known as brimstone or 'burning stone' because it burns, giving a blue flame. Never try to light it, though, because it gives off a poisonous gas. You can find out more about safety on page 2. Pure sulphur is bright yellow. You can sometimes see crusts of it around hot volcanic springs and volcanic chimneys known as fumaroles. Most commercial sulphur, however, is obtained by injecting hot water into sulphur beds in limestone and gypsum to melt it and pump it to the surface.

MINERAL IDENTIFIER

Type: Sulphur
Crystal system: Orthorhombic
Habit: Masses, crusts and powder
Colour: Yellow
Streak: Whitish yellow
Lustre: Glassy or earthy
Hardness: 2
Cleavage: Poor
SG: 2.0-2.1

Diamond

Diamond is one of the world's hardest substances. It is carbon, like coal, but glitters like glass when cut and polished because it has been altered by huge pressures. Diamonds can be made **artificially**, but natural diamonds formed deep underground at least a billion years ago. They were carried to the surface in pipes of hot magma that cooled to form kimberlites and lamproites. Diamonds may be forced out of veins by weathering and washed into streams.

Graphite

Like diamond, graphite is made of carbon, but is very different. It is dull, dark grey and very soft because it is often made from tiny flakes that slide over each other. It's usually found

SULPHIDES OF IRON, LEAD AND ARSENIC

Sulphides are compounds of sulphur with a metal. This is why they often have a metallic look. They include some of the world's key metal ores, such as iron, lead and arsenic ores, and are often heavy and break easily. They usually form in hydrothermal veins or from magmas.

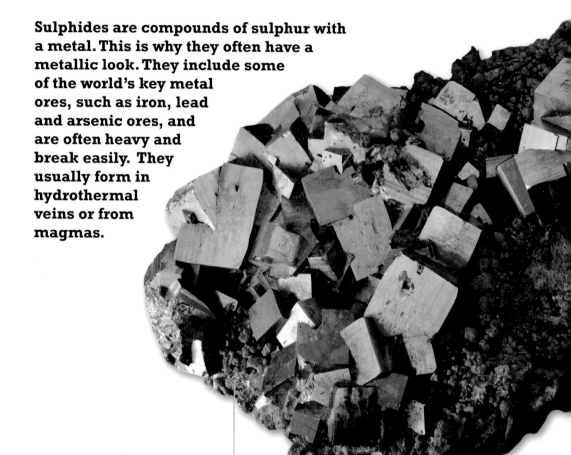

MINERAL IDENTIFIER

Type: Pyrite
Crystal system: Isometric
Habit: Includes cubic crystals and nodules
Colour: Brassy yellow
Streak: Greenish black
Lustre: Metallic
Hardness: 6-6.5
Cleavage: Poor
SG: 5.1+

Pyrite

Pyrite, iron sulphide, is known as 'fool's gold' because it is sometimes mistaken for gold. It is found in most rocks, and any rock that has a 'rusty' look probably contains pyrite. It gives off sparks when struck against metal, which is why people used it as a firelighter in ancient times.

MINERAL IDENTIFIER

Type: Marcasite
Crystal system: Orthorhombic
Habit: Bladed crystals or massive
Colour: Pale yellow
Streak: Greenish brown
Lustre: Metallic
Hardness: 6-6.5
Cleavage: Poor in two ways
SG: 4.8+

Marcasite

Marcasite is iron sulphide and looks like pyrite. But unlike pyrite, it changes colour and crumbles when exposed to air. You usually find it near surfaces where acid solutions trickle down through shale, clay and limestone.

Galena

Galena is the main ore of lead. It contains only tiny traces of silver, but so much galena is mined that it is also the main source of silver. It usually forms in hydrothermal veins along with pyrite, sphalerite and chalcopyrite. It is easy to identify from its cubic, dark grey crystals.

MINERAL IDENTIFIER

Type: Galena
Crystal system: Isometric
Habit: Typically cubic crystals
Colour: Dark grey
Streak: Lead grey
Lustre: Metallic to dull
Hardness: 2.5+
Cleavage: Perfect in four ways
SG: 7.5-7.6

Orpiment and realgar

Orpiment and realgar are very attractive sulphides. Orpiment is buttery yellow, and realgar is orangey-red. However, beware! They are both ores of the poisonous metal arsenic. Like arsenic, they both smell of garlic. If you accidentally touch them, you must wash your hands afterwards.

MINERAL IDENTIFIER

Type: Orpiment
Crystal system: Monoclinic
Habit: Flaky or pillared masses and crusts
Colour: Yellow
Streak: Yellow
Lustre: Resinous, pearly
Hardness: 1.5-2
Cleavage: Forms flakes
SG: 3.5

SULPHIDES OF ZINC, MERCURY AND COPPER

The main ores of zinc, mercury and copper are dug from the ground in huge quantities to be sold to businesses. But you can still sometimes find beautiful crystals of zinc, mercury and copper sulphides to add to your collection.

Sphalerite

The main ore of zinc, sphalerite often looks like galena, and often forms with it and with pyrite. It can also come in black (known to miners as 'black jack'), red (known as 'ruby jack') and other colours. The best clue to its identity is its yellowish-beige streak.

MINERAL IDENTIFIER

Type: Sphalerite
Crystal system: Isometric
Habit: Tetrahedral and dodecahedral crystals
Colour: Black, brown, red, green
Streak: Buff
Lustre: Adamantine, resinous
Hardness: 3.5-4
Cleavage: Perfect in six ways
SG: 4

MINERAL IDENTIFIER

Type: Stibnite
Crystal system: Orthorhombic
Habit: Sprays of needles
Colour: Steel grey, silver
Streak: Dark grey
Lustre: Metallic
Hardness: 2
Cleavage: Perfect lengthways
SG: 4.5-4.6

Stibnite

Stibnite is the ore for the metal antimony, which is used to improve the strength of lead and tin. Stibnite forms amazing needle-like crystals.

MINERAL IDENTIFIER

Type: Cinnabar
Crystal system: Trigonal
Habit: Rhombohedral crystals
Colour: Red
Streak: Red
Lustre: Adamantine
Hardness: 2-2.5
Cleavage: Perfect in three ways
SG: 8.1

Cinnabar

Cinnabar is the main ore for mercury. Usually bright scarlet, its name means 'dragon's blood' in ancient Persian. It was once used to make the red paint pigment, vermilion.

Chalcopyrite

Chalcopyrite is the main ore for copper, and forms in veins and pegmatites. When tarnished, its surface shimmers greens, blues and purples, which is why it is known as 'peacock copper'. Underneath, the pyramid-shaped crystals are like a yellowish pyrite.

MINERAL IDENTIFIER

Type: Chalcopyrite
Crystal system: Tetragonal
Habit: Masses, or tetrahedral crystals
Colour: Yellow, tarnishing turquoise
Streak: Dark green
Lustre: Metallic
Hardness: 3.5-4
Cleavage: Poor
SG: 4.2

MINERAL IDENTIFIER

Type: Bornite
Crystal system: Isometric
Habit: Mostly masses
Colour: Flesh pink, tarnishing turquoise
Streak: Grey-black
Lustre: Metallic
Hardness: 3
Cleavage: Very poor
SG: 4.9-5.3

Bornite

Like chalcopyrite, bornite is a copper ore often called 'peacock copper' because of its colours when tarnished. When untarnished, bornite is pink.

OXIDES

There is so much oxygen in the Earth that nearly every mineral contains some. But geologists call only those minerals that are a metal combined with oxygen 'oxides'. There are many oxides, since every metal except gold and silver combine with oxygen. Oxides include widespread bauxite (aluminium ore) and rare gems, like sapphires and rubies.

MINERAL IDENTIFIER

Type: Rutile
Crystal system: Tetragonal
Habit: Needle masses and eight-side prisms
Colour: Reddish brown
Streak: Brown
Lustre: Adamantine
Hardness: 6-6.5
Cleavage: Good in two ways
SG: 4.2+

Rutile

Rutile gets its name from the German for red, since it has a coppery tinge. But it is actually titanium oxide, and the most important ore of titanium. It is famously found in pockets called 'vugs' in the Swiss Alps. It can be found as needle-like crystals, but is best known for forming tiny needles inside gems such as ruby and sapphire.

Perovskite

Another titanium ore, perovskite, makes up most of the Earth's mantle, so is probably the world's most **abundant** mineral. But it is rarer on the surface and was only discovered in 1839, in the Russian Ural mountains. If you see dark, box-shaped crystals in rocks such as syenites and volcanic pipes, it is probably perovskite.

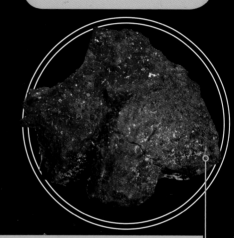

Cuprite

If you see a ruby red mass covered with bright green, it is likely to be cuprite. Cuprite is a common ore of copper that forms when other copper minerals are exposed to the air. This is why it is often found near the surface. You usually find it mixed with iron oxides in earthy lumps.

Haematite

Haematite gets its name from the Ancient Greek for 'blood', because it gives rocks and soils a blood-red tinge. It is the most important ore for iron and usually occurs in earthy masses called red ochre. It can also form kidney-shaped lumps in pockets called 'iron roses'.

OXIDE GEMS: RUBIES, SAPPHIRES, SPINEL

Most oxide minerals are earthy and a bit boring to look at. But, in very special circumstances, they can form beautiful gems – rubies, sapphires and spinel. Most are actually the aluminium oxide mineral corundum, but slight differences in the way they form, and traces of other chemicals, create huge variations in colour.

Corundum

Corundum is one of the hardest minerals of all. Corundum is so hard that when crushed into a black powder called emery, it is often used to sharpen knives. When it forms crystals, pure corundum is brown and translucent.

MINERAL IDENTIFIER

Type: Corundum
Crystal system: Hexagonal
Habit: Powdery masses, or six-sided crystals
Colour: Brown or black
Streak: White
Lustre: Vitreous
Hardness: 9
Cleavage: None
SG: 4+

Ruby

Ruby is one of the most stunning of all gems. It gets its fabulous red colour from traces of chromium. Rubies start out embedded in marble, but because they are so hard, they survive after the marble is worn away.

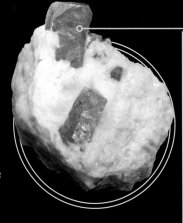

Sapphire

For geologists, a corundum gem of any colour that is not a ruby is a sapphire. For jewellers, only bright blue gems are sapphires. They are coloured blue by traces of the titanium oxide mineral, almenite. The most famous sapphires are from Kashmir, India.

Spinel

Spinels are a large group of oxide minerals that contain various metals, including magnesium and aluminium. The best known is the gem form. Gem spinel can be a red that is almost as rich as ruby, green, turquoise or black. It forms in metamorphic rocks such as marble and gneiss, and in pegmatites.

SALTS

When a metal combines with one of the five elements called halogens, such as chlorine and fluorine, a mineral called a halide is formed. Halides look a bit like coloured salt, and they are known as salts. The most common, called halite, is also called rock salt. Like table salt, these salty minerals dissolve in water, which is why many are only found in very dry places, such as the Great Salt Lake in Utah, United States.

MINERAL IDENTIFIER

Type: Halite
Crystal system: Isometric
Habit: Cubic or hopper crystals
Colour: Clear or white, occasionally pink or blue
Streak: White
Lustre: Vitreous
Hardness: 2
Cleavage: Perfect in three ways
SG: 2.1+

Halite

Halite, or rock salt, is sodium chloride. Much of the salt we use on our food comes from halite. It is mined from thick underground beds that formed long ago, when oceans evaporated in very hot conditions. Crystals are usually cubic, but you may see rare 'hopper' crystals with a dent in one side.

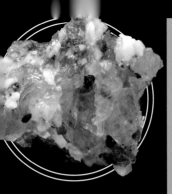

Sylvite

Sylvite is similar to halite, but is potassium chloride, rather than sodium chloride. It is a major source of **potash** for **fertilizers**. Over a quarter of the world's supply comes from Saskatchewan in Canada. Halite turns to a powder if you cut it, while sylvite does not.

Fluorite

Fluorite is basically calcium chloride, and only contains a little fluorine. Fluorite is useful for helping melt metal and glass. It is also used in dental products, such as toothpaste. It forms a fabulous range of coloured crystals, but is so fragile that it is rarely used as a gem. It often fluoresces, or glows, when exposed to short-wave light, such as ultraviolet.

Blue John is a purplish blue and yellow striped fluorite. The name Blue John simply comes from the French *bleu jaune,* meaning blue yellow.

CARBONATES

A carbonate mineral is formed when a metal or semi-metal joins with carbon and oxygen. Most carbonates form when other minerals on the surface are changed by the slight acidity of the air. They tend to be pale, soft and brittle. There are over 80 different kinds of carbonate, including the calcites and the aragonites.

Calcite

Calcite is one of the world's most common minerals. It is the crust that forms in kettles and around taps, and is a key ingredient in marbles and limestone. It often forms fantastic dripstone formations in caves. Calcite crystals, too, take on all kinds of different shapes. Iceland spar are amazingly clear crystals of calcite that look like pieces of ice.

MINERAL IDENTIFIER

Type: Calcite (Iceland spar)
Crystal system: Trigonal
Habit: Mostly masses
Colour: Clear or white
Streak: White
Lustre: Vitreous
Hardness: 3
Cleavage: Perfect in three ways
SG: 2.7

Rhodochrosite

While calcite and other carbonates are pale coloured, rhodochrosite can be a rich pink.

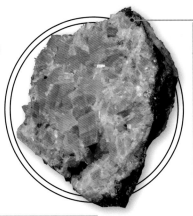

MINERAL IDENTIFIER
Type: Rhodochrosite
Crystal system: Trigonal
Habit: Masses, druses and stalactites
Colour: Rose pink
Streak: White
Lustre: Vitreous
Hardness: 3.5-4
Cleavage: Perfect in three ways
SG: 3.5

MINERAL IDENTIFIER
Type: Aragonite
Crystal system: Orthorhombic
Habit: Prisms and wedges
Colour: White or clear
Streak: White
Lustre: Vitreous
Hardness: 3.5-4
Cleavage: Distinct one way
SG: 2.9-3

Aragonite

Aragonites include witherite and cerussite. Cerussite, also known as white lead, is an important source of lead. Common aragonite is a mineral that sea creatures use to make their shells. Stalactites and crusts around hot springs are often aragonite as well. Aragonite is hard to tell apart from calcite.

Malachite

Malachite is verdigris, the green tarnish on copper and bronze. It forms green masses when carbonated water comes into contact with copper. Malachite is usually found as round masses with dark and pale rings.

MINERAL IDENTIFIER
Type: Malachite
Crystal system: Monoclinic
Habit: Rounded masses, or tufts of needles
Colour: Green
Streak: Pale green
Lustre: Vitreous to dull
Hardness: 3.5-4
Cleavage: Rare
SG: 4

MINERAL IDENTIFIER
Type: Azurite
Crystal system: Monoclinic
Habit: Velvety masses or needles
Colour: Deep blue
Streak: Sky blue
Lustre: Vitreous to dull
Hardness: 3.5-4
Cleavage: Good in one way
SG: 3.7+

Azurite

Azurite is created by the weathering of copper minerals, turning blue because its crystals contain water. During the 15th and 16th centuries, ground azurite was used by artists to make paints.

SULPHATES, CHROMATES AND PHOSPHATES

Sulphates are a group of about 200 minerals made from a metal combining with sulphur and oxygen. They are usually formed by the weathering of sulphides, and are soft, pale-coloured and often transparent. Chromates and phosphates are similar, but they have chromium and phosphorus instead of sulphur. They include beautiful crystals of crocoite and wulfenite.

Barite

Barite is a very dense mineral that is used for helping to bring oil to the surface in oil wells. It also forms amazing tabular (tablet-like) crystals, and crested forms that look like roses, known as 'Cherokees' tears'.

MINERAL IDENTIFIER

Type: Barite
Crystal system: Orthorhombic
Habit: Various
Colour: Clear or white
Streak: White
Lustre: Vitreous
Hardness: 3-3.5
Cleavage: Perfect in one way
SG: 4.5

Celestite

Celestite is easy to recognize from its delicate sky blue colour. It can look a little like blue barite but is often associated with fossils such as ammonite.

MINERAL IDENTIFIER

Type: Celestite
Crystal system: Orthorhombic
Habit: Various
Colour: Usually blue
Streak: White
Lustre: Vitreous
Hardness: 3-3.5
Cleavage: Perfect in one way
SG: 4

Gypsum

Gypsum is a common mineral that forms thick, soft white beds where salty water evaporates. It is used to make plaster and cements, and, when hard, can form the white stone, alabaster. Selenite is a variety of gypsum.

MINERAL IDENTIFIER

Type: Gypsum
Crystal system: Monoclinic
Habit: Massive beds, blocks of alabaster and crystals of selenite
Colour: White or clear
Streak: White
Lustre: Vitreous
Hardness: 2
Cleavage: Distinct in one way
SG: 2.3+

Crocoite

Crocoite gets its name from the crocus flower that produces the orange-red spice, saffron. The metal chromium gives it splinter-like, saffron-coloured crystals. It was once an ore of chromium but is now too rare. The Dundas mines in Tasmania were once famous for crocoite.

MINERAL IDENTIFIER

Type: Crocoite
Crystal system: Monoclinic
Habit: Splinter-like clusters
Colour: Orange-red
Streak: Orange-yellow
Lustre: Adamantine to greasy
Hardness: 3.5-4
Cleavage: Distinct in two ways
SG: 6+

MINERAL IDENTIFIER

Type: Wulfenite
Crystal system: Tetragonal
Habit: Thin square crystals
Colour: Orange yellow
Streak: White
Lustre: Vitreous
Hardness: 3
Cleavage: Perfect in one way
SG: 6.8

Wulfenite

The chemical name for wulfenite is lead molybdate. It was named after the **mineralogist** Xavier Wulfen who discovered it in Austria in 1785. Its strange crystals look almost like piles of plastic counters.

6 SILICATE MINERALS

Silicates are the most abundant minerals on the Earth's surface. They make up nearly half of the most common minerals. The igneous rocks that cover more than 90 per cent of the Earth's crust are made up almost entirely of silicates. Most silicate minerals are tough and long-lasting, and often survive long after the rock in which they were formed has worn away.

Under a microscope, you can see the varied silicate skeletons of diatoms, which pile up as sediments on the seabed when they die.

How do silicates form?

Some silicate minerals formed when metamorphic or sedimentary rocks were made. Most, though, were first created when magmas cooled to become igneous rocks. They were later re-made into other rocks. The skeletons of tiny sea creatures called diatoms are made of silicates, too. When tiny diatoms die, their skeletons pile up in a sandy slime on the ocean bed.

Silicate groups

Silicate **molecules** are built around a basic pyramid. Silicates are divided into groups by the way atoms attach to this pyramid to form different shaped molecules.

Phyllosilicate molecules (such as micas): sheets

Nesosilicate molecules (such as garnets, olivine and topaz): simple pyramid

Cyclosilicate molecules (such as beryl and tourmaline): rings

Oxygen atoms

Silica atom

Sorosilicate molecules (such as epidote): double pyramid

Silicates are built up from pyramid-shaped molecules. Four oxygen atoms join with one silica atom.

Inosilicates (such as pyroxenes and amphiboles): chains

Tectosilicate molecules (such as quartz): complex framework

Sheet silicates

The molecules of phyllosilicates, such as micas and clay minerals, are sheets. This is why these minerals are often flaky and soft. Phyllosilicate minerals are important in soil. Their sheet structure allows space for air to get into the soil and stops it from being waterlogged.

Phyllosilicates help soil take up and hold water, making room for animals and plants to live and grow there.

QUARTZ

Quartz is by far the most common mineral on Earth. It is the main ingredient in most igneous and metamorphic rocks, and even in sedimentary rocks like sandstone. It is so tough that its chunks and grains last long after these rocks have disintegrated. Pebbles, gravel and sand on beaches are all mostly quartz. Pure quartz is dull and colourless, but impurities turn it into a stunning range of coloured gems.

DID YOU KNOW?

A red and white banded form of chalcedony (see below right) known as sardonyx was once thought the most precious gem of all by the Ancient Romans.

Common quartz

Quartz is found mostly as tiny grains inside rocks such as granite, which formed when magmas rich in silica and water became crystallized. However, larger and often beautiful crystals of quartz form in special conditions, such as in crusts, hydrothermal veins and in **geodes** in sandstone. Rose quartz is a common pink gem form of quartz. It gets its colour from rutile.

Mineral Identifier

Type: Rose quartz
Crystal system: Trigonal
Habit: Variable, but often forms hexagonal prisms
Colour: Pink
Streak: White
Lustre: Vitreous or resinous
Hardness: 7
Cleavage: Poor
SG: 2.65

Mineral Identifier

Type: Amethyst
Crystal system: Rhombohedral
Habit: hexagonal prism ending in hexagonal pyramid
Colour: Purple, violet
Streak: White
Lustre: Vitreous or glossy
Hardness: 7
Cleavage: Poor
SG: 2.65

Amethyst

Amethyst gets its purple colour from traces of iron. The largest amethysts come from Brazil and Uruguay where they form in giant geodes big enough to climb into.

Citrine

Citrine is a yellow quartz gem that gets its colour from tiny grains of iron oxide. It looks like topaz but is softer. Citrine gems you can buy are often not citrine at all, but have been made by heating amethyst until it turns the same colour as citrine.

Mineral Identifier

Type: Citrine
Crystal system: Trigonal
Habit: Variable, but often forms hexagonal prisms
Colour: Yellow, gold, orange
Streak: White
Lustre: Vitreous
Hardness: 7
Cleavage: Poor
SG: 2.65

Chalcedony

Chalcedony may well be the most widely used gem of all. A crystalline form of sedimentary rock called chert, it looks like coloured glass and can be chipped to give the same sharp edges as glass. It was used thousands of years ago to make the first blades.

Mineral Identifier

Type: Chalcedony
Crystal system: Trigonal
Habit: Cryptocrystalline
Colour: Many colours
Streak: White
Lustre: Vitreous or resinous
Hardness: 7
Cleavage: Poor
SG: 2.65

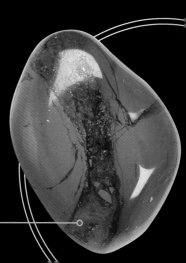

TOURMALINE, BERYL AND TOPAZ

Traces of certain chemicals turn silicate crystals into beautiful gems – tourmaline, beryl and topaz. Even the tiniest traces of other chemicals can transform tourmaline and beryl into other gems – emerald, elbaite and morganite.

Tourmaline

If you find bluish-black, or green and pink crystals flecked with other colours, they may be tourmaline. Tourmaline comes in many different colours, often in the same crystals. This is why the Ancient Egyptians called it 'rainbow rock'. Rainbow colours and a triangle-shaped cross-section mean it is probably tourmaline. Tourmaline forms in granite veins and where limestone is metamorphosed by granite magma. If you are lucky, you may find these gems in river gravel near granite areas.

Mineral Identifier

Type: Tourmaline
Crystal system: Trigonal
Habit: Typically hexagonal prisms
Colour: Variable, commonly black or bluish black
Streak: White
Lustre: Vitreous
Hardness: 7.5
Cleavage: Very poor
SG: 3-3.2

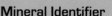

Beryl

Beryl forms deep in the Earth, frozen in masses of quartz feldspar. It also forms from mineral-rich water in cavities. In caves in Colombia, beryls can grow as big as telegraph poles. You can identify 'proper' beryl from its hard hexagonal red and golden crystals. Traces of chrome and vanadium turn beryl into green emeralds. Blue beryl is called aquamarine, yellow beryl is heliodore and pink beryl is morganite.

Mineral Identifier

Type: Beryl
Crystal system: Hexagonal
Habit: Hexagonal prisms
Colour: Wide range from gold to pink
Streak: White
Lustre: Vitreous
Hardness: 7.5-8
Cleavage: Poor
SG: 2.6-2.9

Mineral Identifier

Type: Topaz
Crystal system: Orthorhombic
Habit: Usually prisms
Colour: Colourless, pale colours such as yellow
Streak: White
Lustre: Vitreous
Hardness: 8
Cleavage: Perfect basal
SG: 3.5-3.6

Topaz

Topaz may have got its name from the **Sanskrit** word for 'fire', or from the legendary island of Topazios in the Red Sea, now known as Zebirget. The best clue to identifying topaz is its exceptional hardness and density, and its range of pale colours such as yellow and pink, especially when found near fluorite in granite pegmatites.

An opal is the one kind of quartz gem that does not form crystals. It is a hardened gel that forms from silica-rich fluids. It looks more like pearl with its pale, shimmering colours.

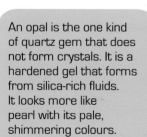

GARNETS AND OLIVINES

Making garnets and olivines requires extremely high temperatures and pressures – the kind of heat you get only deep inside the Earth or where mountain roots have been metamorphosed. These gems are very rare but tough and beautiful.

Garnet

Garnet is the general name for over 20 minerals including green andradite, purple-red almandine and ruby-red spessartine. Garnets usually form in metamorphic rocks such as schists and gneisses. Sometimes they can form so close together in peridotite that the rock is studded with red gems, like a cherry cake. Grossular garnet is a kind of garnet found in marble that looks like gooseberries

Mineral Identifier

Type: Garnet (spessartine)
Crystal system: Isometric
Habit: Rhombic or trapezoid
Colour: Typically red or green
Streak: White
Lustre: Vitreous
Hardness: 6.5-7.5
Cleavage: None
SG: about 3.8

Pyrope

Pyrope is a red, ruby-like garnet. It gets its name from the Greek for 'fire' and 'eye'. You may see it embedded in dunite and peridotite. It is also found in kimberlite pipes, along with diamonds. Red almandine can look a little like pyrope, but pyrope is generally a deeper red. Like all garnets, you are most likely to find pyrope gems in river gravels, though they are rare.

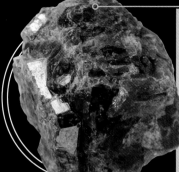

Mineral Identifier

Type: Pyrope
Crystal system: Isometric
Habit: Rhombic or trapezoid
Colour: Red
Streak: White
Lustre: Vitreous
Hardness: 6.5-7.5
Cleavage: None
SG: 3.5

Mineral Identifier

Type: Olivine
Crystal system: Orthorhombic
Habit: Short prisms
Colour: Olive green
Streak: White
Lustre: Vitreous
Hardness: 6.5-7
Cleavage: Poor
SG: about 3.5

Olivine

Olivine gets its name from its green olive colour. It is made when minerals rich in iron and magnesium are cooked at high temperatures. It is a key ingredient of the rock peridotite. Near the surface, olivine is found as tiny, rare grains in basalt and gabbro. It can form large, very rare gems called peridote.

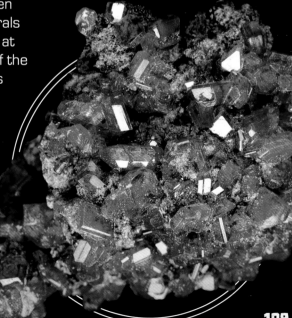

Garnets got their name because red garnet looks like pomegranate seeds.

FELDSPARS

There are two kinds of feldspar – potassium (K) or orthoclase feldspar, and plagioclase (sodium and calcium) feldspar. Together, they are even more abundant than quartz. In fact, these two feldspars make up more than two-thirds of the Earth's crust. Orthoclase feldspar is one of the main ingredients in granite and many other igneous and metamorphic rocks.

Mineral Identifier

Type: Orthoclase
Crystal system: Monoclinic
Habit: Typically massive but may form tablet-shaped crystals
Colour: Off-white
Streak: White
Lustre: Vitreous
Hardness: 6
Cleavage: Good in two directions
SG: 2.53

Orthoclase

Our homes are full of orthoclase. As one of the main ingredients in porcelain, it is what makes our cups and bowls, mugs and plates. The orthoclase used in porcelain is mostly the massive form found in rocks such as aplite. But it can also form tabular crystals. Moonstones are rare orthoclase gems with a shimmering coloured surface.

DID YOU KNOW?

The precious gemstone lapis lazuli (see right) probably gets its name from the Latin word for stone, 'lapis', and the ancient Arabic word for sky, 'azul'.

Albite and anorthite

Unlike orthoclase feldspars, plagioclase feldspars, such as albite and anorthite, often form in **twinned** crystals. Twinning is particularly common in albite. But you can often only tell the difference between plagioclases by working out the specific gravity. Albite has the most sodium; anorthite the most calcium. The others, such as oligoclase, lie in between.

Mineral Identifier

Type: Albite
Crystal system: Triclinic
Habit: Mostly massive, but forms crystal twins
Colour: Off white
Streak: White
Lustre: Vitreous
Hardness: 6-6.5
Cleavage: Good in two directions
SG: 2.63 (albite), 2.76 (anorthite)

Lazurite

Blue lazurite's chemical make-up is complicated. Its blue colour comes from sulphur. Masses of lazurite are ground to make the paint pigment ultramarine. Lazurite is also a major ingredient in lapis lazuli, one of the oldest and most treasured of gems.

Mineral Identifier

Type: Lazurite
Crystal system: Cubic
Habit: Masses or hexagonal column crystals
Colour: Blue
Streak: White
Lustre: Greasy to dull
Hardness: 5.5-6
Cleavage: Poor
SG: 2.6

Lapis lazuli was first mined over 6000 years ago at Sar-e-Sang in the Kotchka valley of Afghanistan. It was a favourite gem of the Ancient Sumerians and Egyptians.

MICA

Silicates that form in sheets are phyllosilicates. There are many of them, and they include clays like kaolin, which is important for making china. They also include micas. These silicate minerals are made when potassium and aluminium link up with silicates. Micas are a key ingredient in granites, gneisses and schists.

Biotite mica

Look at a chunk of granite, and you'll see lots of tiny black dots, like grains of pepper. The black dots are usually biotite mica, which is why it is often called black mica. When separate from granite, mica flakes into thin sheets. Mica only occasionally forms crystals.

Mineral Identifier

Type: Biotite mica
Crystal system: Monoclinic
Habit: Flaky grains
Colour: Brown or black
Streak: White
Lustre: Vitreous to pearly
Hardness: 2.5
Cleavage: Perfect in one way
SG: 2.9-3.4

Mineral Identifier

Type: Muscovite
Crystal system: Monoclinic
Habit: Flaky grains
Colour: Brown or black
Streak: White
Lustre: Vitreous to pearly
Hardness: 2.5-3
Cleavage: Perfect in one way
SG: 2.9

Muscovite

White mica is called muscovite. It gets its name from the old name for Russia, Muscovy, where thin, almost transparent sheets of mica were once used to make windows instead of glass. Now it is used to make artificial snow.

MINERALOIDS

Not all solid substances that form naturally in the Earth are minerals. When living things are fossilized, it can create substances such as amber and jet. Amber and jet are as beautiful as any gems, but are not made from crystals, so are not minerals. They are known as mineraloids.

Amber

Amber looks like solid orange honey or a boiled sweet. It is actually the solidified **resin** of trees that lived millions of years ago. It is usually found in dense, wet sediments such as clay and sand, formed in lagoons and river beds.

Mineral Identifier

Type: Amber
Crystal system: None
Habit: Nodules and droplets
Colour: Amber
Streak: White
Lustre: Resinous
Hardness: 2+
Cleavage: None
SG: 1.1

Jet and coal

Jet is shiny black. Like amber, jet and coal come from trees that lived long ago. Coal forms from the **compressed** remains of ancient swampy forests. Jet was made from logs that floated out to sea and sank to the seabed.

Mineral Identifier

Type: Jet (below right), coal (above right)
Crystal system: None
Habit: Lumps
Colour: Black
Streak: White
Lustre: Glassy
Hardness: 2-2.5
Cleavage: None
SG: 1.1-1.3

GLOSSARY

Abundant Produced in large amounts.

Acidic rock Igneous rock formed from magma that contains a lot of silica.

Algae Simple plants that live mostly in water and are so tiny they can only be seen under a microscope.

Artificially Made by humans, not by nature.

Assemblages Masses of different minerals that form together.

Associations Minerals that naturally occur together.

Atoms The smallest bits of any chemical element.

Avalanches Huge masses of snow, ice and rocks that rush down slopes.

Biochemical rocks A rock formed from the remains of living things or by chemical processes.

Calcium carbonate A substance made up of calcium, oxygen and carbon that occurs naturally in chalks, limestones and marble.

Carbon One of the most important elements on Earth and comes in many forms, including diamond, graphite and black coal.

Cavities Holes

Cement A powdery substance, which, when mixed with water, hardens and sticks other materials together.

Chaotic Lacking in order.

Characteristics Features belonging to something that help you to identify it.

Chemical elements Simple substances that can't be broken down into any simpler substances.

Chemicals Substances with a particular set of molecules.

Clastic rocks Rocks made from the pieces of other rocks.

Clusters Groups or clumps.

Compacted Squeezed into a smaller space.

Compounds Substances that combine two or more chemical elements.

Compressed Pressed or squeezed together.

Contaminated Made impure, or unclean, by adding other materials.

Continental crust The thick part of the Earth's crust that forms continents.

Continents Very large land masses on the Earth's surface.

Corals Colourful sea creatures with a hard skeleton.

Corrode Worn down or weakened by chemicals.

Crystallize Form crystals.

Crystals Tiny particles, or grains, that interlock like a jigsaw inside most minerals.

Current Flow of water in one direction, such in as in a river.

Dense Closely packed together and heavy.

Deposits Places where stones are found lying loose, such as beaches, river beds and fields.

Detergent A substance used for cleaning, such as washing-up liquid.

Disintegrated Broken up into tiny pieces.

Dissolves When a solid mixes with and becomes part of a liquid.

Dykes Wall-like formations of igneous rock formed by the injection of magma into a vertical (upright) crack in the ground.

Electric currents Flows of electric charge through a material.

Embedded Fixed firmly in a surrounding mass.

Erupt When a volcano suddenly throws out material on the surface.

Evaporate Turn from liquid to vapour, such as water to steam.

Fertilizers Extra nutrients added to crops to keep them healthy and help them grow better.

Fissures Long, narrow cracks.

Fossilized When a living thing is preserved by being turned to stone.

Fragments Small, broken off parts of something.

Fringes Outside edges.

Fuels Materials, such as coal and gas, that are burned to produce heat or power.

Gems Rare, richly coloured crystals that are hard enough to cut and shape into jewels.

Geodes Small cavities in rocks lined with crystals.

Geological To do with the study of rocks and minerals.

Geologists Scientists who study rocks.

Glaciers Slow-moving rivers of almost solid ice.

Gorges Deep, narrow passages of rock with steep sides.

Grains Small, hard crystals that make up rocks and minerals.

Hydrothermal solutions Hot, watery fluids rich in minerals that bubble up from magma.

Hydrothermal veins See **veins**.

Hypabyssal rocks an igneous rock usually formed at a shallow distance below the surface.

Igneous rock Rock formed by the cooling of hot liquid magma.

Impurities Substances that are not pure and contaminate other substances.

Insoluble Cannot be dissolved.

Karst Typical limestone scenery, with gorges, caves and slabs of rock.

Lagoons Lakes formed from the sea.

Landslide Sudden collapse of part of a cliff.

Lava Molten magma that has erupted from a volcano.

Lava dome A circular mound created by the slow oozing of lava from a volcano.

Lens A body of rock that is thick in the middle and thin at the edges.

Local Happening over only a small part of the surrounding area.

Magma Hot molten rock that comes from the Earth's interior.

Magnetic Materials such as iron that are pulled or pushed apart by the force of magnetism.

Mantle The vast layer of the Earth between the thin crust and the core.

Margins Outside edges.

Mass A large collection or formation of something.

Melt Melted rock.

Metamorphic Rock that has been formed by the alteration of others by extreme heat and pressure.

Metamorphosed When rock is altered by extreme rock and pressure.

Mineralogist A scientist who studies minerals.

Minerals Naturally occurring solids, usually crystal.

Molecules The smallest particle of a chemical that normally exists by itself.

Molten Turned to liquid by extreme heat.

Native elements Minerals formed only of a single element, for example, gold or silver.

Ores Rocks containing metals that can be extracted (taken out), and used in building or for making useful products.

Organic Made from living things.

Outcrops Places where bare rock appears in the landscape.

Plankton A huge group of tiny plants or animals that float in water near the surface.

Plutonic When rocks form from magma that has cooled and turned solid deep below the ground.

Potash Salts that contain the chemical potassium.

Precipitated out When a solid emerges from a liquid solution.

Preserved Kept or stored safely for a long period of time.

Pressure When something pushes on something.

Quarries Large holes in the ground where rocks, such as slate, are dug out to use as building material.

Recrystallize Crystallize again.

Replica An exact copy.

Resin A sticky fluid often formed from tree sap.

Rift The crack between two tectonic plates that are pulling apart.

Rust A reddish brown coating on a metal that forms after it has come into contact with the air or moisture.

Sanskrit The ancient language of India.

Schistosity The stripiness of metamorphic rocks that have been put under extreme heat and pressure.

Scree A pile of broken rock at the base of a cliff.

Sedimentary rock
Rock formed by the piling up of mineral and organic fragments that have been dropped by water or wind.

Sediments Layers of mineral and organic fragments dropped by water, wind or ice.

Semi-metals Brittle solids that are half way between a metal and a non-metal.

Sequence Layers of rocks arranged in a particular order.

Shoals Groups

Silicates The most common group of minerals on the Earth.

Sills Sheet-like formations of igneous rock formed by the injection of magma into a horizontal (level) crack in the ground.

Silt A fine, sand-like substance that settles at the bottom of a river or seabed.

Solidified Turned solid.

Solutions Mixtures made when a solid mixes into a liquid.

Species A type of animal or plant.

Specimens Rock samples

Stalactites An icicle-shaped mineral formation that hangs from the roof of caves, formed from the dripping of mineral-rich water.

Stalagmites A pillar of mineral deposit that rises from the floor of caves.

Streak The colour left by a mineral when you rub it across the back of a white tile.

Subduction zones Areas where one tectonic plate has been forced under another.

Substance Any kind of material, such as rocks, powders and liquids.

Tar A black substance often used for covering road surfaces.

Tarnishes Loses its shine or colour when exposed to air.

Terranes Parts of the landscape formed by a fragment of tectonic plate.

Transparent
See-through

Transport Move to a different area.

Tropical Of, or from the tropics.

Twinned Two crystals that share some of the same symmetry.

Untarnished A rock or mineral that has kept its normal colour and shine.

Valley A low area of land that is surrounded by higher land, usually with a river or stream running through it.

Veins Cracks in the rock filled with mineral-rich fluid that has gone hard.

Volume Amount of space a solid or liquid takes up.

Weathered out Rocks broken down by rain water, wind and extreme heat and cold.

Weather resistant
The ability of a rock or mineral to be unchanged when exposed to wind, rain, snow, heat or cold.

INDEX